Safe Living in a Dangerous World

Also by Nancy Harvey Steorts:

Safety and You (Syracuse University Press, 1999)

Safe Living in a Dangerous World

An Expert Answers Your Every Question From Homeland Security to Home Safety

Nancy Harvey Steorts

Former Chairman, U.S. Consumer Product

Safety Commission

CAPITAL
BOOKS, INC.
Sterling, Virginia

Capital Books, Inc.
P.O. Box 605
Herndon, Virginia 20172-0605

ISBN 1-931868-44-1 (alk.paper)

Library of Congress Cataloging-in-Publication Data
Steorts, Nancy Harvey, 1936-
  Safe living in a dangerous world : an expert answers your every
question from homeland security to home safety / Nancy Harvey Steorts.
      p. cm.
Includes bibliographical references and index.
  ISBN 1-931868-44-1
  1. Terrorism—Prevention—Government policy—United States. 2.
National security—United States. 3. Civil defense—United States. 4.
Emergency management—United States. 5. Dwellings—Security
measures—United States. 6. Schools—United States—Defenses. I. Title.

HV6432.S738 2003
613.6—dc21

                                  2002155655

Printed in the United States of America on acid-free paper that meets the American National Standards Institute Z39-48 Standard.

First Edition

10 9 8 7 6 5 4 3 2 1

This book is dedicated to each of you. May you find answers to your questions and may you find solace in being prepared. Knowing what to do is extremely helpful when we are facing so many uncertainties in this world.

And, to my dear daughter, Deborah, and my very cherished grandson, Madison, who are both so special to me. May they, and those you cherish, be safe from harm and live long, productive lives.

ACKNOWLEDGMENTS

It is with deep gratitude that I recognize the special contributions of many who have helped bring *Safe Living in a Dangerous World* to reality.

In my first book, *Safety and You*, I said thank you to those individuals who opened so many doors in my life and allowed me to make a difference in society. Since September 11, 2001, however, there has been a great awakening in our country to the reality that we can no longer take our lives for granted. We have been taught to live each day to its fullest, regardless of the difficulties, and to be extremely grateful to those who are always there to help us as we journey through life.

In this book, therefore, I want to say a heartfelt thank you to all those who have made—and continue to make—such a difference in our society today: from our first responders, the firefighters, medics, and policemen who are always there when there is an emergency, to our medical community, the nurses, doctors, and hospital technicians, who are always on the scene to care for us if we are injured or have a medical problem.

It is so very important that I recognize my colleagues in the government, who are constantly reviewing our products and services to be sure they are safe and free from hazard. May I point out a few: the

Food and Drug Administration, the U.S. Consumer Product Safety Commission, the U.S Department of Agriculture, the Department of Health and Human Services, the Department of Transportation, and the newest agency—the Department of Homeland Security. We should also recognize our governors, attorneys general, and mayors, who at the state and local levels are constantly monitoring the safety of their citizens against injury and potential terrorism.

I want to recognize my colleagues in the media for bringing national and local attention to very important safety issues. Many reporters have diligently covered these issues and made the public aware of conditions that have caused grave injury and death to innocent victims. Now that homeland security is so very much on our minds, the media is bringing the issue of personal security to our attention as well. I have appeared on many of their programs, and I know how important these programs are to listening audiences. I especially want to thank my colleagues at Channel 21 in the Washington, D.C., area, who have given me the opportunity to present a regular weekly segment on safety issues to their viewing audience for the last several years.

This book would not have been completed in a timely fashion without the support of three very important individuals. First, let me recognize my outstanding colleague, Stephen Ingram, who has worked so diligently with me over the last ten years. With Stephen's excellent organizational skills and attention to detail we were able to organize this material in a manner that I know will be helpful to the reader. Thank you, Stephen, for a job well done.

Amy Johnston, a longtime friend, was extremely proficient in editing several chapters of this book, greatly improving its readability. Her expertise and her knowledge of change management, organization reengineering, and strategic planning—as well as her editorial skills—have added greatly to this book.

Lane Kemmerick Jordan first worked with me as an intern when she was a senior at the University of Georgia. Now a graduate, Lane contributed a great deal of material to the college safety tips, and contributed much to the final edit. Thank you, Lane, for all of your hard work and for keeping me on deadline.

In conclusion, I must say a very special thank you to Kathleen Hughes and her wonderful team at Capital Books. Thank you for your vision and confidence in bringing this very important book to the marketplace.

CONTENTS

Part 4: The External World

Introduction

Preparing for a Disaster: Are You Ready?

Americans' sense of safety is forever changed after the tragedies of September 11, 2001. Our first reactions to the unbelievable terrorist attacks on the World Trade Center, the Pentagon, and the passengers aboard the plane that crashed in Pennsylvania were those of shock, disbelief, and anger. Suddenly, as debris was falling, buildings were collapsing, flames were out of control, and thousands of people were desperately trapped, we wondered about our families, neighbors, friends, and colleagues. Where were they? Were they safe? How could we reach them?

Brave firefighters, medics, and police officers became our new heroes. They were on the front lines that day and at every emergency in the days that followed. But all of us wanted to help in any way we could. In those hours of sheer terror and panic, people responded, and thousands of lives were saved. We were all as one that day. We were united. Even now we have found new purpose. As we stand united, we will survive.

Today, each of us is looking for ways to do things differently. We are learning how to survive in a seemingly much more dangerous world.

We are looking for ways to protect our loved ones and ourselves. While firefighters, medics, and police officers are our first responders, they cannot be everywhere at once. *We* must help. Every citizen needs to be prepared, to know what to do in case of an emergency.

After September 11, President George W. Bush asked all Americans to be vigilant and to take new responsibility for ourselves, our families, and our neighbors. Part of this work must be to educate ourselves, gain knowledge, and learn new skills to help us live more safely, to help us prevent or mitigate potential threats to our safety. We can use this new information and these new skills to protect our neighborhoods, our institutions, and of course, our families.

Not only must we now prepare for potential terrorist attacks, but each of us must also learn how to avoid everyday accidents in our homes, schools, or neighborhoods as well as how to protect ourselves against acts of nature such as tornadoes, earthquakes, unexpected snowstorms, heat waves, and rainstorms that clog drains and make rivers out of normal streets. We must learn how to travel more safely and how to protect our loved ones when they are away from home.

Former United Nations Ambassador Jeane Kirkpatrick said in a recent speech, "What we are encountering today is as different a time as we have ever encountered. The emergence of terrorism makes this a peculiarly dangerous time. . . . Educating all Americans to be safe and prudent is extremely important. One must have an appreciation for danger, which needs to start with education at home."

Safety is everyone's responsibility. We must work together, assume new responsibilities, and learn new ways to protect ourselves, our families, our communities, and our country. As we learn new ways to live safely, we will all benefit. We will begin to reduce injuries and deaths related to external threats and all other threats around us.

This book is part of that effort. May it help you and your family be safe.

PART 1

HOMELAND SECURITY

1

America's Response to New Challenges

 "We can never be overconfident about the security of our homeland," said President George W. Bush soon after the events of September 11. He called them "a harsh wake-up call to all citizens, revealing to us the dangers we each face. Our American values and our way of life have been threatened. . . . Securing our homeland is a national priority."

Virtually every American responded to the terrorist attack on September 11. We helped first responders and victims. We tried to save lives, comfort families, minister to the sick, set up aid stations, help in our communities, and assist in the long, arduous recovery efforts. We were courageous, responsible, and concerned for others. America continues to respond in an overwhelmingly positive way to what is a terrifying new challenge. That response must not stop.

President Bush has summoned everyone to be part of the solution. Governors, mayors, county officials, health and medical officials, community organizations, corporations, students, and church groups are all playing a role in securing our homeland. State, county, and local authorities are working together. Citizens are forming volunteer organizations to make America safer. Local governments are purchasing new equipment and training volunteers in all aspects of safety to build the expertise to respond to the next terrorist attack.

President George W. Bush announced a nationwide effort to involve Americans in service activities to make their communities safer and better prepared to respond to national and local emergencies. There are several ways that we can do our part to ensure our safety from external threats.

Education is one of the most important components in meeting this challenge. Senate Majority Leader Bill Frist, a surgeon by training, warns: "The goal is not to frighten Americans but to educate them, empower them, and stir them to action. . . . We need to be deputized into action. Every citizen needs to learn how to be prepared. We need a national call to action, so each person will know what do. We need to know what to do in an emergency, so citizens can feel comfortable with what they can do or will do if an emergency should occur. We need to learn how to take care of each other. We must be proactive, not reactive."

Homeland Security

In the past, when we talked about safety, we were concerned with the personal safety of consumers. Since September 11, 2001, however, we are experiencing threats from outside forces—inside our own borders. These are truly threats to the security of our entire country. President Bush called for the establishment of a new federal agency to coordinate "defense" strategies at home.

In 2003 the new Department of Homeland Security was established. This vast federal agency is responsible for developing and implementing a comprehensive strategic plan for defending our homeland against enemy attacks. The head of that department, Secretary Tom Ridge, has said: "By working together, federal, state and local government, with the medical profession, schools, fire, police, and first responders, corporations, volunteer organizations, and hundreds of other community-based organizations we can protect America, and we can protect our people. This is a massive undertaking, but we can and will be ready. Each one will teach one. We will be prepared and we will survive. We will mobilize, we will train, and we will communicate."

As a first act, the Homeland Security Advisory System was established to warn government and the public regarding the risk of terrorist acts. This color-coded risk-warning system alerts us to the level of a potential terrorist threat. There are five threat conditions. Each one is identified by a description and corresponding color. From the lowest to the highest levels of risk, the conditions are:

Risk Level	Color Code	Conditions Described
Low	Green	Low risk of terrorist attacks
Guarded	Blue	General risk of terrorist attacks
Elevated	Yellow	Significant risk of terrorist attacks
High	Orange	High risk of terrorist attacks
Severe	Red	Imminent risk of terrorist attacks

The level of risk includes both the probability of an attack occurring and its potential gravity. Threat conditions may be assigned for the entire nation, or for a particular geographic area or industrial sector. The assignment of a threat condition prompts the implementation of an appropriate set of protective measures. The decision on announcing threat conditions is made by the president, who is advised by the secretary of the Department of Homeland Security.

A New Threat to Safety: Bioterrorism

Secretary of the Department of Homeland Security Tom Ridge has said, "We must be prepared to deal with the notion that terrorist attacks are a permanent condition. They can strike at any time. The terrorist threat to America takes many forms, has many places to hide, and is often invisible." Bioterrorism is one of the most frightening new threats to our safety.

Since the end of World War II, we as average citizens have not been prepared for such a terrible, and potentially destructive, personal threat. As Senate Majority Leader Bill Frist has explained, "The risk of a bioterrorist attack is real, and the risk is increasing. . . . We are underprepared as a nation. . . . The effort for preparedness needs to be focused at the state and local level. We must learn about biological agents; we must be prepared."

That said, our nation is confronting this challenge. As has occurred when public safety was threatened in the past, federal, state, and local governments and the private sector are working on ways to deter, manage, and recover from a bioterrorist attack.

The Homeland Security Advisory System is an early warning system of such a threat. Now we need to be able to deal with the medical consequences should one occur. The first step is to improve public health-care systems, the best means to deal with biological attacks as well as potential epidemics. This requires providing new vaccines and medical equipment and supplies, as well as research on how to respond to attacks.

In 2002 U.S. Secretary of Health and Human Services Tommy Thompson said that we "have the greatest opportunity to build a public health system that will make our nation safer, protect our lives, and strengthen America." This program is what safety is all about: recognizing a threat, mobilizing resources, stakeholders working together, and putting together a response to better protect us.

Our Role

After a terrorist attack, properly trained and equipped first responders—firefighters, medics, and police—have the greatest potential to save lives and limit casualties. Increased financing and equipment is being made available to them. But at the local level, citizens will be called to actively participate in preparing their towns for the threat of terrorism and other such disastrous events in the following ways.

First, get educated. Learn about the new vaccines, therapeutics, and diagnostic tests and about what health problems might be posed by various bioterrorist attacks. We must do our own research and be ready to share our knowledge with our health-care provider.

Second, expect more drills, more "mock evacuations." By being prepared and going through a drill, we will be better able to determine what to do if it is the "real thing." This is what being prepared is all about.

An emergency drill is staged each year at the Pentagon. In the early spring of 2001, just a few months before September 11, Air Force Colonel John Baxter suggested that the Pentagon have a drill for a possible 757 aircraft crashing into the Pentagon. Although this was a mock drill, it taught hundreds of Pentagon employees what to do in case of such a disaster. Because of his foresight many lives were saved when the real disaster took place.

Finally, education and emergency drills are two parts of the entire disaster response equation, which also includes preparation and practice. Everyone should develop emergency response plans and prepare Disaster Emergency Supplies Kits. The rest of this chapter, like the entire book, contains detailed and specific actions to take to prepare for, respond to, and recover from disasters, emergencies, and other dangers. Become familiar with the response plans designed to ensure the safety of you and your loved ones. Think about your safety in the context of concentric circles: you have responsibilities first to yourself, then to your family and friends, and finally to your neighborhood and community. You, like everyone else, have a role to play. This book talks about safety issues and challenges at all levels of our lives today and offers ways to keep you, your family and friends, and your community safe.

"Don't Be Afraid. . . . Be Ready"

The U.S. Homeland Security Agency urges: "Don't be afraid. . . . Be ready." In this new era where we are faced with many terrible threats, protecting ourselves and our homeland is vital. Some threats seem so remote it is hard to make serious preparations. But the use by terrorists of weapons of mass destruction is not only possible, it is inevitable. In the face of such danger, how can we protect ourselves from biological, chemical, radiological, and even nuclear weapons?

Biological

A biological weapons attack would spread infectious agents such as bacteria and viruses. These include anthrax and smallpox. Biological agents can be dispersed through aerosol sprays, which, for a large-scale attack, might involve a low-flying plane with specially equipped canisters or, for a low-scale attack, might involve a small aerosol canister aboard a subway train or bus or in an enclosed space. Biological agents, like chemical agents, could also be used to contaminate food or water supplies.

To prepare for a biological weapons attack, take the following precautions, which are taken from the Federal Emergency Management Agency's (FEMA) "Are You Ready? A Guide to Citizen Preparedness":

- Put together an emergency supplies kit, described elsewhere in this book
- Have sanitation supplies, such as soap and water, readily available.
- Procure duct tape and plastic to use on doors, windows, and vents to keep out hazardous air.

If a biological attack ever occurs, take the following actions:

- Listen to radio or other transmitting devices to get instructions from local authorities.
- Seek shelter in your dwelling by going to an internal room with few windows, doors, or vents; turn off ventilation; and use duct tape and plastic to secure the room if necessary. Make sure the room is large enough to ensure fresh air for at least five hours for each person who will be using the accommodation. The standard is ten square feet per person.
- If outside, stay upwind of attack location and follow previous instructions.

To recover from an attack, it is important to realize that you won't know at first if you have been exposed. The best advice is to monitor media broadcasts, follow briefings by local authorities of "mysterious" outbreaks of illness, and if you are concerned, contact your local hospital or health authority. For more information about diseases, symptoms, and treatments, access the Centers for Disease Control website at www.cdc.gov.

Chemical

Although somewhat like biological weapons in their effect, chemical weapons are basically poisonous substances that can be in varying forms, including liquids, solids, and vapors. They can be dispersed through bombs and aerosol nozzles from aircraft or used to contaminate food or water supplies. The six types of agents, according to a FEMA publication, are pulmonary, cyanide, vesicants or blister, nerve, incapacitating, and riot-control.

To prepare for and/or take action during a chemical attack, follow the aforementioned instructions for biological attacks. To recover from a chemical weapons attack, follow these recommendations:

- Remove any clothing or accessories that may have come into contact with the body.
- Wash face and hair with plenty of soap and water, and flush eyes out with water.
- Change into clothes that are not likely to have been contaminated, probably clothes in drawers or closets.
- Go to a medical facility for further assistance.
- If you are assisting someone else who might have been contaminated, follow the same instructions, being particularly careful not to contaminate yourself.

Nuclear or Radiological

Perhaps most frightening are nuclear or radiological attacks; however, the latter one is likely to result in less damage and fewer injuries than may be assumed. Radiological weapons combine conventional explosives with radioactive material and cause a significantly smaller amount of damage than a nuclear explosion. This type of attack would result in sublethal amounts of radiation but would probably incite panic among the public. A nuclear attack would probably involve a suitcase-sized device with explosive energy on a par with World War II devices.

There are certain guidelines to follow to prepare for, respond to, and recover from these types of attacks.

For biological, chemical, or nuclear attack, you are better protected through the use of heavy shielding (rooms with thick walls), putting distance between you and the fallout (such as an underground area), and the passage of time (radiation intensity declines to 1 percent of its original level after two weeks).

To prepare for these types of attacks, consider the following measures:

- Know the warning signals and emergency communication channels.

- Put together an emergency supplies kit.
- Identify nearby shelters.
- If in a tall building or apartment complex, seek shelter. Contact your on-site supervisor for assistance.
- Learn about community and neighborhood response plans.

During an attack:

- Do not look at any flash or fireball.
- Take cover as quickly as possible.
- Remember Shielding, Distance, and Time protective factors.
- Listen to radio transmissions for emergency instructions.

After an attack, the recovery effort must begin. Here is what to do afterwards:

- Do not leave shelter until safe.
- Maintain sanitation as thoroughly as possible.
- Ration water and food if necessary.
- Cooperate.
- When returning home, be alert for possible dangers such as gas leaks or electrical shorts, structural damage, or fires.

Please keep in mind that the previous tips are just an overview. There are many more details contained in official government publications such as those mentioned above from FEMA, the CDC, and the Department of Homeland Security. It is imperative that you do further research until you feel knowledgeable and comfortable enough to respond automatically during an emergency.

2

WHAT YOU CAN DO

 While the U.S. Department of Homeland Security organizes defense activities at the federal level, many exciting community involvement programs are already in place. By activating volunteers all over America to help the professionals, we will be ready for whatever lies ahead.

The Citizens Corps, a component of President George W. Bush's USA Freedom Corps initiative, provides opportunities for individuals to volunteer and participate in local emergency preparation, prevention, and response activities. They include the following:

- Community Emergency Response Team (CERT) Training
- Medical Reserve Corps
- Neighborhood Watch
- Volunteers in Police Service (VIPS)

As a member of the Citizens Corps, you can volunteer your energy and skills to support your local emergency, crime, and natural disaster prevention, preparedness, and response capabilities.

Local Citizens Corps units are coordinated by a Citizens Corps Council composed of local elected officials, first responders, educational institutions, medical facilities, faith-based and community organizations, and civic, business, and industry leaders. They are charged with developing community action plans, assessing threats, identifying resources, and building a web of volunteer support for first-responder activities by drawing on existing programs in their communities and helping to create new ones.

For further information, check out <http://www.fema.gov> or go to the Citizen Corps website, <http://www.citizencorps.gov>.

Your Children, Home, Neighborhood, and Community

In addition to doing your part to help increase safety in your city or community, get involved in your neighborhood.

Your Children

It is vital that adults take time to teach children how to be safe and how to respond in the event of an emergency. Here are ways that you can help improve the security of children.

- ☐ Talk with your children about what to do in case of an emergency.
- ☐ Practice emergency procedures with your children.
- ☐ Tell children about 911 and when to call.
- ☐ Have children let you know as soon as they return from school or their activities.
- ☐ If possible, give a child a cell phone to use only in an emergency.
- ☐ Give your children contact cards with their address and phone number, your work number(s), and the phone numbers of a neighbor and a relative.
- ☐ Have your children call your contact numbers to let you know where they are and that they are safe in the event of an emergency.

☐ Have a predetermined contact place for children to go in
case of an emergency, for example, a school, church,
police department, or firehouse.

Your Home

You and your family spend a large part of your time in your home, so
knowing how to respond in the event of an emergency is critical. Follow these suggestions to put together an emergency response plan
and maintain safety at your home.

☐ Always carry with you a card with important contact
numbers, as well as your name, address, workplace, and
information on your children's schools and activities and
all other specific places you regularly frequent.

☐ Design a family emergency plan that states whom you will
call, how you will call, and how you will get there if necessary.

☐ Have an out-of-town contact everyone can call and report
to, if necessary.

☐ Be sure everyone has a contact list with all numbers on it.

☐ Provide prepaid phone cards to everyone who does not
have a cell phone.

☐ Identify places close to home and some distance away to
meet in case of a major emergency.

☐ Have an emergency supply kit in your car, office, and
home.

☐ Always keep your gas tank at least half full.

☐ Take a CPR first aid training course.

Your Neighborhood

In an environment of potential disasters, both man-made and natural, you and your neighbors need to develop an action plan to follow in responding to emergencies and helping individuals who may be most vulnerable. Get to know your neighbors and find out what skills each person may be able to contribute. Follow these steps to create an action plan.

- ☐ Work with your neighbors to devise a plan for emergencies.
- ☐ Include contact information for emergency service providers.
- ☐ Make your home address visible, so that emergency workers can find your home more easily.
- ☐ Contact the American Red Cross <http://www.redcross.org>, 1-866-438-4636, or the Federal Emergency Management Agency (FEMA) <http://www.fema.gov>, 1-800-480-2520, for more information about disaster plans.
- ☐ Take a Red Cross CPR and first aid training course, so you can aid people in need.
- ☐ Organize a neighborhood help program, so that everyone who has specific skills that might be helpful in an emergency can be activated.
- ☐ Designate emergency block captains in neighborhoods and emergency floor captains in high-rise buildings. These captains would be responsible for organizing emergency responses.
- ☐ Observe all fire alarms and evacuate buildings. Assume it is a fire, not a false alarm.

Your Community

Just as with a neighborhood, individuals must take steps to improve a community's response to any emergency. Here are some ideas to implement.

- ☐ Develop a list of emergency services and their phone numbers, including schools, churches, police, fire department, shelters, Red Cross, food bank.
- ☐ Work with community organizations to develop their emergency disaster plans.
- ☐ Start a neighborhood watch group.

Your Work

On September 11, 2001, many people were at work or were getting ready to arrive. Every place of business should have safety plans, and you should do your part by knowing how to respond in an emergency situation. Follow these suggestions to create a response plan and maintain safety at your workplace.

- ☐ Practice the plan carefully, so you will be prepared in case of an emergency.
- ☐ Learn all exit routes in the building.
- ☐ Know at least two exit routes from each room in case there should be a blockage at one.
- ☐ If possible, carry a flashlight.
- ☐ Count the number of desks and cubicles between your office or workstation and the exits.
- ☐ Have a specified meeting place outside the building designated where everyone can be accounted for and missing workers can be identified.
- ☐ Make special emergency plans for disabled coworkers during an emergency. Know where fire extinguishers and medical kits are located.
- ☐ Have your own emergency kit with all necessary supplies.
- ☐ Carry a list of important phone numbers with you at all times.

- ☐ Always carry a charged cell phone.
- ☐ Do not block any fire exit or stairway. Keep fire doors closed to slow the spread of the fire and smoke.

Evacuation of a High-Rise Building

To evacuate a high-rise building safely, follow these instructions for leaving the building or waiting until first responders arrive to assist you.

- ☐ Leave the building quickly.
- ☐ Do not use an elevator.
- ☐ Test doors for heat before opening them.
- ☐ In case of fire, crawl under the smoke for cleaner air.
- ☐ If you are trapped in a building, stay calm. Wrap a towel around your face to protect yourself from smoke inhalation. Go to a room with a window and telephone for help.
- ☐ Stay where rescuers can see you.
- ☐ Wave a light cloth to attract attention.
- ☐ Blow a whistle to attract attention.
- ☐ Be careful about opening windows. If there is smoke present, opening a window can create a draft that draws the flames closer. A wiser step is to follow the next suggestion to prevent smoke from entering. Also, keep in mind that smoke always rises, so stay low.
- ☐ If possible, to prevent smoke from entering the room, stuff clothing, towels, or newspaper around cracks in doors.
- ☐ Set up a telephone tree to enable employees or residents to be quickly notified of emergencies. Be sure you have home phone numbers.
- ☐ Help each other in any way that you can.

Your Family Disaster Supplies Kit

After a disaster, local officials and relief workers will be on the scene, but they cannot reach everyone immediately. You could get help in hours, or it may take days. Would your family be prepared to deal with the emergency until help arrives?

Your family can cope best by preparing for disaster before it strikes. One way to prepare is to assemble a disaster supplies kit. With the items contained in this kit in hand, your family can better endure an evacuation or home confinement.

There are seven basics you should stock in your home: water, food, first aid supplies, tools and supplies, clothing and bedding, sanitation basics, and special items. Keep the items you would most likely need during an evacuation in an easy-to-carry container. These items are marked in the following listings with an asterisk (*). Possible containers include a large, covered trash container, a camping backpack, or a duffle bag.

Water

Store water in plastic containers. Avoid using containers that will decompose or break, such as paper cartons or glass bottles. A normally active person needs to drink at least two quarts of water each day. Hot environments and intense physical activity can double that amount. Children, nursing mothers, and ill people will need more.

☐ Store one gallon of water per person per day (two quarts for drinking, two quarts for food preparation/sanitation).*

☐ Keep at least a three-day supply of water for each person in your household.

Food

Store at least a three-day supply of nonperishable food. Select foods that require no refrigeration, preparation, or cooking and little or no water. If you must heat food, pack a can of sterno. Select food items that are compact and lightweight.

Include a selection of the following foods in your disaster supplies kit:

- ☐ Ready-to-eat canned meats, fruits, and vegetables
- ☐ Canned juices, milk, and soup (if powdered, store extra water)
- ☐ Staples—sugar, salt, pepper
- ☐ High-energy foods—peanut butter, jelly, crackers, granola bars, trail mix
- ☐ Vitamins
- ☐ Foods for infants, elderly people, or those on special diets
- ☐ Comfort/stress foods—cookies, hard candy, sweetened cereals, lollipops, instant coffee, tea bags

First Aid Kit

Assemble a first aid kit for your home and one for each car. A first aid kit should include:

- ☐ Sterile adhesive bandages in assorted sizes
- ☐ Two-inch sterile gauze pads (four to six)
- ☐ Four-inch sterile gauze pads (four to six)
- ☐ Hypoallergenic adhesive tape
- ☐ Triangular bandages (three)
- ☐ Two-inch sterile roller bandages (three rolls)
- ☐ Three-inch sterile roller bandages (three rolls)
- ☐ Scissors
- ☐ Tweezers

- ☐ Needle
- ☐ Moistened towelettes
- ☐ Antiseptic
- ☐ Thermometer
- ☐ Tongue blades (two)
- ☐ Tube of petroleum jelly or other lubricant
- ☐ Assorted sizes of safety pins
- ☐ Cleansing agent/soap
- ☐ Latex gloves (two pairs)
- ☐ Sunscreen
- ☐ Nonprescription drugs
- ☐ Aspirin or nonaspirin pain reliever
- ☐ Antidiarrhea medication
- ☐ Antacid for an upset stomach
- ☐ Syrup of ipecac to induce vomiting if advised by the poison control center
- ☐ Laxative
- ☐ Activated charcoal to use if advised by the poison control center

Contact your local American Red Cross to obtain a basic first aid manual.

Tools and Supplies

For your family disaster supplies kit, gather the following tools and supplies.

- ☐ Mess kits, or paper cups, plates, and plastic utensils*
- ☐ Emergency preparedness manual*
- ☐ Battery-operated radio and extra batteries*
- ☐ Flashlight and extra batteries*
- ☐ Cash or traveler's checks, change*
- ☐ Manual can opener, utility knife*

- ☐ Fire extinguisher: small canister, ABC type
- ☐ Tube tent
- ☐ Pliers
- ☐ Tape
- ☐ Compass
- ☐ Matches in a waterproof container
- ☐ Aluminum foil
- ☐ Plastic storage containers
- ☐ Signal flare
- ☐ Paper, pencil
- ☐ Needles, thread
- ☐ Medicine dropper
- ☐ Shutoff wrench, to turn off household gas and water
- ☐ Whistle
- ☐ Plastic sheeting
- ☐ Map of the area (for locating shelters)

Clothing and Bedding

Include at least one complete change of clothing and footwear per person.

- ☐ Sturdy shoes or work boots*
- ☐ Hat and gloves
- ☐ Rain gear*
- ☐ Thermal underwear
- ☐ Blankets or sleeping bags*
- ☐ Sunglasses

Sanitation Basics

Ensure that you have adequate supplies to provide for basic sanitation and hygiene.

- ☐ Toilet paper, towelettes*
- ☐ Soap, liquid detergent*
- ☐ Feminine supplies*
- ☐ Personal hygiene items*
- ☐ Plastic garbage bags, ties (for personal sanitation uses)
- ☐ Plastic bucket with tight lid
- ☐ Disinfectant
- ☐ Household chlorine bleach

Special Items

Remember family members with special needs, such as infants and elderly or disabled persons.

For Baby*
- ☐ Formula
- ☐ Diapers
- ☐ Bottles
- ☐ Powdered milk
- ☐ Medications

For Adults*
- ☐ Heart and high blood pressure medication
- ☐ Insulin
- ☐ Prescription drugs
- ☐ Denture needs
- ☐ Contact lenses and supplies
- ☐ Extra eyeglasses
- ☐ Entertainment—games and books
- ☐ Important family documents

Records (Kept in a Waterproof, Portable Container)
- ☐ Wills, insurance policies, contracts, deeds, stocks and bonds

- [ ] Passports, social security cards, immunization records
- [ ] Bank account numbers
- [ ] Credit card account numbers and companies
- [ ] Inventory of valuable household goods, important telephone numbers
- [ ] Family records (birth, marriage, and death certificates)

Suggestions and Reminders

Follow these suggestions to maintain your family disaster supplies kit.

- [ ] Store your kit in a convenient place known to all family members. Keep a smaller version of the disaster supplies kit in the trunk of your car.
- [ ] Keep items in airtight plastic bags.
- [ ] Change your stored water supply every six months so it stays fresh.
- [ ] Rotate your stored food every six months.
- [ ] Rethink your kit and family needs at least once a year. Replace batteries, update clothes, and so forth.
- [ ] Ask your physician or pharmacist about storing prescription medications.

A Family Disaster Plan

Contact your local emergency management or civil defense office and your local American Red Cross chapter for the following information:

- [ ] Find out which disasters are most likely to happen in your community.
- [ ] Ask how you would be warned.
- [ ] Find out how to prepare for each.

☐ Meet with your family to discuss the types of disasters that could occur; explain how to prepare and respond; discuss what to do if advised to evacuate.

☐ Practice what you have discussed.

☐ Plan how your family will stay in contact if separated by disaster.

☐ Pick two meeting places: a location a safe distance from your home in case of fire and a place outside your neighborhood in case you can't return home.

☐ Choose an out-of-state friend as a "check-in contact" for everyone to call.

☐ Post emergency telephone numbers by every phone.

☐ Show responsible family members how and when to shut off water, gas, and electricity at main switches.

☐ Install a smoke detector on each level of your home, especially near bedrooms; test monthly and change the batteries two times each year.

☐ Contact your local fire department to learn about home fire hazards.

☐ Learn first aid and CPR. Contact your local American Red Cross chapter for information and training.

The Federal Emergency Management Agency's Community and Family Preparedness Program and the American Red Cross Disaster Education Program are nationwide efforts to help people prepare for disasters of all types. For more information, contact your local or state office of emergency management and your local American Red Cross chapter. Ask for "Your Family Disaster Plan" and the "Emergency Preparedness Checklist." Or write to: FEMA, P.O. Box 70274, Washington, D.C. 20024, FEMA L-189 ARC 4463. Check the Department of Homeland Security site at www.ready.gov.

PART 2

PERSONAL SECURITY

3

HOME SAFETY: HOW SAFE IS YOUR HOME?

A three-year-old girl was sent by her mother into another room to find a movie to watch. A short time later the mother heard a crashing sound and found a thirty-six-inch television on top of the child. The child had tried to climb up the television stand to reach a movie. The television tipped over because it was too big for the stand.

A seven-year-old boy slipped and fell in a bathtub while taking a bath and required several stitches to his lip.

A company recalled 394,000 electric blankets because the electrical connection could become loose and pose a fire hazard.

A mother and her daughter had to move out of their house for a couple of weeks when wool carpet was installed in their home. Mothproofing chemicals made breathing difficult for them.

The home is where we spend most of our time and is the focal point of our lives. It is where we live, raise children, and grow old. In our homes we eat, sleep, watch television, entertain, celebrate holidays, and do so many other things. It is where we expect to feel safe and secure. It is where we expect our families to be safe. When our kids return home from school, we want them to be safe. The last thing we want to worry about when we are at home is the potential for danger. Our home not only must provide physical shelter, but it must also be a refuge from the dangers of the outside world. Yet, because we spend so much of our lives at home, the chance for being injured there is significant.

We may not realize the dangers that lurk in our homes. The threats in the home are not always obvious and can be very subtle. A loose rug, a sharp edge on a piece of furniture, a window cord, or even our clothing can pose dangers to our loved ones and ourselves. The danger may even exist in the air we breathe. Carbon monoxide, a poisonous, odorless, and colorless gas, is just one pollutant that diminishes indoor air quality and can result in injury or death.

One subtle danger is chemically treated carpet. If someone in your family has respiratory or allergy problems, the cause could be no farther than the carpet under your feet. I know that this is possible because it happened to me. A few years ago I remodeled my house and installed new carpets. Shortly after installation, I developed a sore throat. At first it seemed minor, but after a week or two, I still had a sore throat and had developed respiratory problems. I always felt better when I left my house, but when I returned home, the symptoms returned and gradually got worse. The day after I returned from a trip, I woke up in the middle of the night unable to breathe. It suddenly became obvious to me. It was the carpet! I immediately left my home and spent the next two-and-a-half months away from home.

I was informed that the problem was the carpeting pad or adhesive used in the installation. Medical tests showed that I had over thirty foreign chemicals in my body! I called everyone to tell them what was happening and got the carpet, matting, and adhesive removed. I was lucky that I found out what was happening to me. My years of product safety experience led me to suspect the carpet, when I could just have assumed that I was suffering from allergies.

This example proves that health problems and other dangers are subtle and lurk everywhere, including our homes. The best guard against dangers in your home is taking preventive action. The best way to take action is to become informed about the hazards in your home.

Checklist: Room-by-Room Home Safety

The following room-by-room home safety checklist from the U.S. Consumer Product Safety Commission will enable you to go from room to room and hazard-proof your house. Take this opportunity now to start making your house safer for you and the people you love and care about.

Your Kitchen

Kitchens can be extremely dangerous for everyone—youngsters and adults alike. Many hazards reside in the kitchen. Loose-fitting long sleeves are prone to catching fire and getting caught on pot handles. Gas appliances can produce deadly amounts of toxic carbon monoxide. Air pollutants may accumulate to unhealthy levels where gas or kerosene appliances are used. Placing or storing noncooking equipment, like potholders, dish towels, or plastic utensils, on or near the range may result in fires and burns. The combination of heat sources and less-obvious hazards such as plastic bags and buckets means that the kitchen deserves special attention.

To prevent these hazards and other ones from occurring, use the following tips to make your kitchen safer:

- ☐ Place anything that may catch fire, such as clothing, towels, curtains, papers, and combustible items, away from heat sources.
- ☐ Avoid wearing loose clothing while cooking. Roll back loose sleeves or fasten them.
- ☐ Never use a gas range or oven to heat your home.
- ☐ Use ventilation fans or open windows to clear out vapors and smoke.
- ☐ Ensure that kitchen ventilation systems or range exhaust systems function properly and are used while cooking.
- ☐ Beware of aluminum cookware that can melt and cause severe burns.
- ☐ Never preheat aluminum cookware on high heat or leave aluminum cookware unattended on a stovetop burner.
- ☐ If an aluminum pan boils dry and melts, turn off the heat and do not pick up the pan until it cools.
- ☐ When mopping the floor, be careful with the bucket, especially with children around.
- ☐ When finished with the chore, place the bucket in a place inaccessible to children.
- ☐ Always keep children under close supervision when they are near the kitchen. (See "Child Safety" section in chapter 9.)

Your Garage

The garage is a unique room, because it is one where people are usually aware to some degree of the existing dangers where cars, tools, chemicals, fuse boxes, circuit breakers, and other things are found. Whether it is good parental intuition or if the message has gotten out, parents do realize that there are dangers here. However, let's review the hazards of this location, because the garage is still a very dangerous place.

Cars, Appliances, and Power Tools
- ☐ Never leave your car running in the garage; carbon monoxide could seep into your home.
- ☐ Make sure that power tools are equipped with a three-prong plug or marked to show double insulation. Replace old tools that don't have either of these things.
- ☐ Examine the grounding features of any three-prong plugs to make sure they are being properly used. The grounding pin should not be removed, and adapters that allow for use in two-prong outlets should not be used. The third prong is there because the appliance must be grounded to avoid electric shock.
- ☐ Ensure that power tools have guards. If they don't, serious injury could result.
- ☐ Check with a service person or an electrician to verify the safety of appliances and tools.

Flammable and Volatile Liquids
- ☐ Verify that containers with flammable or volatile liquids are tightly capped and properly labeled.
- ☐ Store gasoline, paints, solvents, and other products that give off vapors or fumes away from heat sources. The U.S. Consumer Product Safety Commission has reports of several cases in which gasoline exploded, even when stored as much as ten feet from a gas water heater.
- ☐ Never store gasoline or other flammable substances in rooms or garages that have heaters, furnaces, water heaters, ranges, gas appliances, or other heat sources. Vapors can travel along the ground and be ignited by pilot lights or electric switches.

Fuse Box and Circuit Breakers
- ☐ Check the fuse box or circuit breakers on a regular basis.

- ☐ Make sure that fuses are the correct size for the circuit. Replacing a fuse with a larger one can present a serious fire hazard, because this allows an excessive current to flow and possibly overload the wiring.
- ☐ Most fuses should be fifteen amps; otherwise, they might be too big for the circuit.
- ☐ If unsure about proper voltage, have an electrician identify and label the correct size.

Lighting

- ☐ Make sure that work areas, especially where power tools are used, are well lit.
- ☐ Ensure that you can turn on the lights without first walking through a dark area.
- ☐ Keep an operating flashlight nearby.
- ☐ Have an electrician install switches at each entrance to a dark area.

Step Stools

- ☐ Make sure that the step stool is stable and in good repair.
- ☐ Verify that the step stool is fully opened before using it.
- ☐ Tighten screws and braces on the step stool periodically.
- ☐ Throw away stools with broken parts.
- ☐ Use a step stool with a handrail that you can hold while standing on the steps.
- ☐ Step on the center of the step, and not near the edge.

Your Living Room or Family Room

The living room can seem quite benign; however, dangers lurk in many places. A particularly dangerous problem is with curtain and window blind cords, which pose strangulation hazards for young children. Furniture such as end tables and coffee tables can be dangerous because of their sharp edges, and doors may slam shut on little fingers. Convertible sofas, easy chairs, or recliners can be dangerous because of how they fold in or out. Fireplaces, of course, pose many hazards.

Electrical Cords

- ☐ Make sure that electrical cords are placed out of the flow of traffic.
- ☐ Do not stretch cords across walkways, because they pose a tripping hazard.
- ☐ Do not place cords underneath furniture or carpeting.
- ☐ Arrange furniture so that the outlets are available for lamps and appliances without having to use extension cords.
- ☐ Use extension cords on a temporary basis only.
- ☐ Move the phone so that people will not walk on the telephone cord.
- ☐ Use cord holders or tape rather than nails or staples to secure cords to walls or floors.

Window Cords for Curtains, Venetian Blinds, and So Forth

- ☐ Keep the cord out of the reach of children.
- ☐ For vertical blinds, continuous loop systems, and drapery cords, install a cord tie-down device. Permanently attach and use the tie-down device.
- ☐ Move cribs or beds away from windows with cords.
- ☐ For horizontal blinds, cut the cord above the tassel, remove the equalizer buckle, and add a breakaway tassel that will separate if a child becomes entangled in the loop.
- ☐ Leave the cord stop near the headrail in place. Cut the cord above the tassel and add a separate tassel at the end of each cord. When shades are raised, a loop will appear above the cord stop.

Fireplaces and Chimneys

Fireplaces

- ☐ Stack firewood toward the back of the fireplace.
- ☐ Do not overload the fireplace with wood.
- ☐ Do not burn garbage, papers, wrapping paper, or anything other than wood in the fireplace.
- ☐ Never leave a fireplace unattended while it is being used.
- ☐ Always watch children around the fireplace and never leave them unattended.
- ☐ Ensure that a protective screen blocks access to the fire and keeps sparks from flying out of the fireplace.
- ☐ Extinguish the fire before going to bed or going out.
- ☐ Install a smoke detector and a carbon monoxide detector in rooms with a fireplace.

Chimneys

- ☐ Clear chimneys of accumulations of leaves and other debris that can clog them. A clogged chimney can result in poisonous fumes and smoke getting into the house.
- ☐ Cut tree branches that hang over the chimney.
- ☐ Install a chimney cap to keep out birds and small animals.
- ☐ Realize that burning wood can cause a buildup of a tarry substance (creosote) inside the chimney. This material can ignite and result in a fire.
- ☐ Have the chimney checked and cleaned by a registered or licensed professional at least once a year.

Furniture

- ☐ Place furniture away from walkways. Furniture can be a tripping hazard.
- ☐ Watch children around furniture with sharp edges or that folds in and out, such as reclining chairs or convertible sofas.

☐ Be sure that all upholstered furniture and fabrics are flame resistant.

☐ Always keep your doors and windows locked when children are around.

Rugs and Mats

☐ Remove rugs and runners that tend to slide, or apply double-faced adhesive carpet tape or rubber matting to the backs of rugs and runners.

☐ Purchase rugs with slip-resistant backing.

☐ Check rugs and mats periodically to see if backing needs to be replaced.

Telephone Area

☐ Post emergency numbers on or near the telephone. Numbers for the police, fire department, poison control center, and a neighbor should be readily available.

☐ Make sure the telephone is accessible in the event of a fall, accident, or other emergency.

Your Bathroom

The bathroom is a very dangerous room. Bathtubs, toilets, and basins are potential danger zones. This room provides a very serious risk of slipping, drowning, and electrocution. Bathtubs and toilets pose a drowning risk for infants. Always be careful when children are in the bathroom. Start by placing all medicines and other potentially dangerous substances out of the reach of children.

Electrical Safety for the Bathroom

☐ Never use an electrical appliance such as a hair dryer, electric razor, or curling iron when water is present.

☐ Do not use an electrical appliance if there is water on the floor or you are in the bathtub or shower.

- [ ] Install a ground fault circuit interrupter (GFCI) that will automatically shut off the electrical current.

Slip Prevention

- [ ] Ensure that bathtubs and showers have mats, abrasive strips, or nonslip surfaces.
- [ ] Place nonslip mats on bathroom floors.
- [ ] If you are unsteady on your feet, use a stool with nonskid tips as a seat while showering or bathing.
- [ ] Always have a night-light turned on in the bathroom.

Grab Bars

- [ ] Install grab bars in showers and bathtubs to assist with getting in and out.
- [ ] Attach grab bars, through the tile, to structural supports in the wall, or install bars specifically designed to attach to the sides of the bathtub. If necessary, get a qualified person to assist you.
- [ ] Check existing bars for strength and stability. Repair, if necessary.

Water Temperatures

- [ ] Lower the setting on your hot water heater to "low" or 120 degrees Fahrenheit. Water temperature above 120 degrees can scald.
- [ ] If unfamiliar with water heater controls, get a qualified person to adjust it.
- [ ] If there is no temperature control, use a thermometer to check the temperature of the water at the tap.
- [ ] Always check water temperature by hand before entering your bathtub or shower.
- [ ] Have a qualified person install a temperature-limiting device on all faucets.

☐ Takings baths rather than showers reduces the risk of scalding from suddenly changing water temperatures.

Your Bedroom

Even bedrooms can be unsafe. Numerous fires have started in bedrooms, especially with cigarettes. Also, because people often have to get up during the night for various reasons, proper lighting is an important consideration in preventing falls or bumps.

☐ Place lamps and light switches within reach of your bed.
☐ Locate ashtrays, smoking materials, or other fire sources such as heaters, hot plates, and teapots away from the bed.
☐ Do not smoke in bed.
☐ Install night-lights.
☐ Never place space heaters, hot liquids, or other heat sources near your bed.

Your Passageways and Stairways

Passageways and stairways can be dangerous when they are not well lit or when obstructions are present.

Passageways

☐ Check hallways and passageways for adequate lighting.
☐ Keep exits and passageways clear.
☐ Remove boxes and clutter from passageways and stairways.

Stairs

☐ Ensure that stairs are well lit.
☐ Have the ability to turn on the lights at either end before using the stairway.
☐ Stairs should be lighted so that each step, particularly the

step edges, can be clearly seen while going up and down stairs.

- ☐ Keep a flashlight in a convenient location at the top and bottom of the stairs.
- ☐ Install night-lights at nearby outlets.

Handrails

- ☐ Make sure that handrails are fastened securely on both sides of the stairway.
- ☐ Install handrails and ensure that they run the entire length of the staircase.
- ☐ Always use the handrail when climbing up or going down the steps.
- ☐ Repair broken handrails.

Steps

Indoor Steps

- ☐ Ensure that the steps allow secure footing.
- ☐ Attach carpet or runners securely to steps.
- ☐ Refinish or replace worn carpeting or runners.
- ☐ Make sure steps are even and of the same size and height.
- ☐ Avoid wearing only socks or smooth-soled shoes or slippers when using stairs.
- ☐ Make sure that steps can be seen clearly; add extra lighting, if necessary.
- ☐ Remove all objects from the stairway.
- ☐ Avoid deep pile carpeting or patterned or dark-colored carpeting that can make it difficult to see the edges of the steps clearly.

Outdoor Steps

- ☐ Paint steps with paint that has a rough texture, or use abrasive strips.

- ☐ Be sure that steps are consistent in size.
- ☐ Mark steps that are especially narrow or that rise higher or lower than the other ones.
- ☐ Repair, remove, and replace broken or damaged steps.
- ☐ Add extra lighting.
- ☐ Remove all objects from the stairway.

Other Safety Areas

Lighting

- ☐ Use the maximum wattage bulb allowed by the fixture. If correct wattage is unknown, use a bulb no stronger than sixty watts.
- ☐ Reduce glare by using frosted bulbs, indirect lighting, or shades.
- ☐ Consider using additional lamps or light fixtures if lighting is inadequate.
- ☐ Fix or get rid of table and floor lamps with frayed electrical wiring.
- ☐ Ensure that wattage used for chandeliers is correct.
- ☐ Ensure that light switches are located near the entrance to each room.
- ☐ Install night-lights.
- ☐ Consider using "glow," or illuminated, switches that can be seen in the dark.

Whirlpools, Hot Tubs, and Spas

- ☐ Make sure that the drain meets American National Standards Institute (ANSI) or American Society of Mechanical Engineers (ASME) safety standards.
- ☐ Keep hair away from the drain cover.
- ☐ Do not allow a child to play in a way that could cause him or her to get caught in the drain. Always supervise children.

- ☐ If the drain cover is missing or broken, do not use until replaced or fixed.
- ☐ Make sure that the water temperature does not exceed 104 degrees Fahrenheit.
- ☐ Pregnant women and children should not use a spa.
- ☐ Use a locked safety cover when the spa is not in use.
- ☐ Have a professional check your spa to make sure it is in good working condition.
- ☐ Check the drain covers throughout the year.
- ☐ Locate the cutoff switch for your pump is so it can be turned off in an emergency.
- ☐ Do not consume alcohol when using the spa.

Conclusion

If you follow these general tips, your home will be safer for you and your family; however, always be vigilant. Accidents still can happen and dangers still may be present. You should periodically hazard-proof your home, using these tips. Many more dangers lurk in almost every place imaginable.

4

FIRE AND ELECTRICAL SAFETY

A fire caused by the ignition of lint from a clothes dryer caused the death of a woman who was in a house full of family and guests.

 Fire kills more people every year than all of the natural disasters in the United States combined. Thousands of people die from fire every year in this country. Most residential fire deaths occur because of inhalation of toxic gases rather than contact with the flames. The tragedy is that these deaths could be prevented by taking a few precautions. The most important way to deal with the threat of fire is to prevent fire from ever occurring. Recognize and eliminate hazards before they have a chance to start a fire.

Safeguarding against Fires

Working smoke detectors along with a well-rehearsed escape plan can mean the difference between life and death. The following covers the most important areas to consider in developing a family home escape plan.

Smoke Detectors

Most home fire injuries and deaths are caused by smoke and toxic gases rather than by the fire itself. Smoke detectors are the best alarm in the event of a fire and provide an early warning that gives you time to escape from your home. Through education and media campaigns, most people now realize the importance of smoke detectors; subsequently, most homes in the United States now have them. They not only save lives, but studies show that money spent on smoke detectors reduces direct and indirect medical costs as well as other costs to society.

Here is a quick checklist to ensure that smoke detectors are used correctly:

- ☐ Purchase smoke detectors if you do not have them already.
- ☐ Smoke detectors should be placed near bedrooms, either on the ceiling or on the wall six to twelve inches below the ceiling. At least one smoke detector should be placed on every floor of your home. Local codes may require more detectors. Check with your fire department or building code official.
- ☐ Locate smoke detectors away from air vents.
- ☐ Test your alarms regularly. Follow manufacturer's directions for testing the detector.
- ☐ Check and replace batteries and bulbs according to the manufacturer's instructions.
- ☐ Change the battery every six months: for example, when the time changes in fall and spring.
- ☐ Clean the smoke detector regularly.
- ☐ Replace any smoke detectors that are broken.

☐ Check with the local fire department or local government for help and/or advice.

Fire Extinguishers

To guard against small fires or to keep a small fire from developing into a big one, you should consider investing in a fire extinguisher. Every home and business should have one. Since almost all fires are small initially, they might be contained if a fire extinguisher is handy and used properly. You should take care, however, in selecting the right kind of fire extinguisher, because different ones are used for different kinds of fires. Also, selecting the right one is necessary to reduce the damage to your possessions from the extinguishing agents.

Selecting a Fire Extinguisher

Extinguishers are classified according to the type of fire for which they are suitable. The four basic types are A, B, C, and D, which are classified as follows:

- Class A: Ordinary materials, such as wood, paper, cloth, and most plastics
- Class B: Flammable liquids and gases, such as gasoline, oils, paint, and greases
- Class C: Electrical equipment
- Class D: Combustible metals

Choosing the Type of Extinguishing Agent

Five common groups of extinguishing agents are available on the market. You should choose one that will handle the correct class of fire.

- Dry Chemical: Useful on Class B and C fires. It leaves a corrosive residue that must be cleaned immediately to prevent damage to electrical equipment. Its best uses are for automotive fires and fires caused by grease and flammable liquids.

- Carbon Dioxide: Useful for Class B and C fires. It is very clean and leaves no residue, but it has a short range and must be applied close to the fire.
- Halogenated Agents: Useful for Class A, B, and C fires, depending on agent used. These extinguishers are expensive, but versatile and clean. Halogenated agents are toxic, but they leave no residue. This extinguisher is excellent for computers and electrical equipment, for fires caused by flammable liquids, and for fires in motor vehicles.
- Multipurpose Type: Useful for Class A, B, and C fires. This type of extinguisher is effective on the most common types of fires; however, it is corrosive and leaves a residue. It should not be used around delicate electrical appliances or computers.
- Water-Based Agent: Use for Class A fires only. It is inexpensive to refill and maintain.

Using a Fire Extinguisher

Fire extinguishers can be used for small fires; however, the fire department should always be called and the area evacuated. The fire department will check to make sure that the fire is completely out, because a small fire that appears to be out may still be burning somewhere, such as behind a wall, where it could spread rapidly. Become familiar with the location, use, and limitations of fire extinguishers in your home or anywhere else you are, such as your place of employment.

Escaping from a Fire

In the event of a fire, an emergency exit plan and an alternate plan are vital. It is also crucial to have two exits in case of an emergency. Be sure that everyone knows what to do. You should formulate an exit plan now, because if a fire occurs, you may not have much time to get out and there may be a lot of confusion. Follow these instructions to formulate an exit plan and to learn how to escape a fire.

Escape Plan

The first thing you should do in your escape plan is to ensure that there are two ways out of each bedroom. A window is usually going to be the second exit. Make sure it is not blocked by furniture and that children know how to raise it. Screens must come off easily. If you have security bars, they must have inside quick-release devices. Practice using them. If you live in a two-story home, you should have a ladder. Have one for each occupied bedroom. They fold into a small box that fits under your bed.

The second thing your family should do is to choose a meeting place outside your home so you can be sure that everyone has escaped. Ensure that it is reasonably far from your home and away from the street.

Third, rehearsing your escape plan regularly is essential. A routine that has been practiced will override panic in an emergency situation. Children who have practiced fire drills at home will automatically do the correct thing in a real emergency. Without such practice, children will usually hide under a bed or in a closet. A small amount of time spent planning and rehearsing your escape plan may mean the difference between life and death.

Finally, you should make sure that you have smoke detectors and that they are working, because they are the keys in providing you with the warning you need to implement the emergency exit plan.

Evacuating

Once awakened by your detector, yell and shout to make sure that all family members are awake.

- ☐ Get out of your home as fast as possible once the alarm has sounded. Do not stop to dress or gather valuables. Don't let the children look for their favorite toys or even the family pet.
- ☐ Test the doors before opening them to make sure it is safe on the other side. Feel the door for heat and look for

smoke seeping in around the edges. If you feel the door is safe to open, then do so slowly and be prepared to slam it shut if heat and smoke rush in.

☐ Make sure that, once out, everyone stays out. As soon as two people have reached the meeting place, one should leave to call 911 at a neighbor's house. The second member should stay to account for all other family members. If someone is missing, do not go back inside; notify responding fire companies immediately upon arrival.

Fires in Apartment Buildings or Hotels

If you live in an apartment building or are staying in a hotel, make sure the smoke alarms are working and that you know how and where to evacuate. Do not take the elevator.

Checklist: Fire Safety General Tips

The following is a fire hazard checklist to help prevent fires from occurring in your home:

☐ Do not use small electrical appliances such as curling irons, radios, and hair dryers close to water.

☐ Do not plug multiple appliances into an electrical outlet.

☐ Make sure that papers, books, clothing, furniture, or curtains are not close to heat sources or anything with an open flame, such as fireplaces, heaters, candles, cigarettes, stoves, ovens, or furnaces.

☐ Don't smoke in bed or leave a cigarette in an ashtray.

☐ Do not use damaged appliances or extension cords.

☐ Place flammable objects, such as matches and lighters, out of the reach of children.

☐ Get smoke detectors and always test them to make sure they are working properly.

☐ Invest in fire extinguishers, particularly for the kitchen, garage, and fireplace.

☐ Do not place furniture in front of any doors that must be clear for escape plans.

☐ Locate space heaters away from passageways and flammable materials such as curtains, rugs, furniture, and newspapers and make sure they are installed properly.

☐ Make sure that space heaters have proper venting and are checked frequently.

☐ Always use the correct fuel for space heaters as recommended by the manufacturer.

Electrical Safety

A child and his sister were playing unattended in a bedroom and knocked a halogen floor lamp onto a bed, which caused a fire. As a result, the child died of smoke inhalation.

Shocks, fires, and electrocutions caused by failures of electrical safety occur thousands of times each year. Electrical safety is therefore very important. Electrical products are ubiquitous and part of modern life. As much as we use electricity, particular care needs to be taken around it. Fortunately, most consumers are already aware of the danger that electricity poses. Although most people know not to use a hair dryer near water, other dangers exist. Taking precautions and using safety devices can reduce the risk of an accident.

Ground Fault Circuit Interrupter (GFCI)

One of the most significant and helpful devices to reduce electrocutions and shocks is the ground fault circuit interrupter (GFCI). The GFCI is an inexpensive electrical device that is specifically designed to prevent shocks, electrocutions, and electrical fires. The GFCI automatically cuts off the electrical current when the risk of a shock or a short is greatest. Household electrical outlets in the bathroom and kitchen and electrical appliances such as hair dryers should have GFCIs installed. The following tips explain how to use and maintain a ground fault circuit interrupter:

Checklist: Ground Fault Circuit Interrupter

- ☐ Install GFCIs on all electrical outlets in your kitchen and bathrooms.
- ☐ Test your GFCIs each month to ensure that they continue to offer protection. A GFCI may continue to provide power but not indicate that it no longer works.
- ☐ To test the GFCI, take the following steps: Plug a night-light or lamp (with the light turned on) into the GFCI receptacle. Depress the "TEST" button on the GFCI. If the GFCI is working properly, the "RESET" button will release and the light will go out.
- ☐ If the "RESET" button releases but the light does not go out, the GFCI has been improperly wired and does not offer shock protection. Contact an electrician to install the GFCI properly.
- ☐ If the "RESET" button does not release, the GFCI is defective and should be replaced.
- ☐ Depress the "RESET" button to restore power to the outlet if the test shows your GFCI is working properly.

Electrical Safety Checklist

Many electrical hazards exist in your home. To reduce the danger, read the following tips from the U.S. Consumer Product Safety Commission:

Electrical Cords

- ☐ Check wiring and cords for damage and replace as necessary.

☐ Use cords within the marked electrical rating.

☐ Change to an extension cord with a higher voltage rating or unplug some appliances if the electrical demands of the appliances used on the cord exceed its rating.

☐ Ensure that extension cords carry no more than their proper load, as indicated by the ratings labeled on the cord and/or appliance.

Light Bulbs

☐ Make sure that light bulbs are the appropriate type, size, and wattage for lamps and fixtures. Ceiling fixtures, recessed lights, and "hooded" lamps trap heat.

Small Electrical Appliances

☐ Unplug small electrical appliances such as hair dryers, shavers, and curling irons when not in use. If they come into contact with water, it could cause a shock or electrocution.

☐ Never reach into water to get an appliance unless the appliance is unplugged.

Outlets and Switches

☐ Install GFCIs in electrical outlets, and purchase appliances with built-in GFCIs.

☐ Unplug cords from outlets and do not use switches if they are unusually warm, because it may indicate unsafe wiring.

☐ Have an electrician check wiring periodically.

☐ Install cover plates over outlets and switches.

Outdoor Electrical Safety Tips

☐ Do not fly kites near power lines. If a kite falls on a power line, don't try to retrieve it or touch the kite string.

☐ Do not cut down or climb trees around power lines.

- [ ] Do not touch fallen electrical wires. All wires on the ground are live and dangerous.
- [ ] Do not climb utility poles, towers, or substation fences.
- [ ] If any of these things happen, call the electric company for assistance.

Electricity is very dangerous but is essential to our society. Through GFCIs and the safety tips mentioned above, hazards caused by electricity can be reduced.

5

Carbon Monoxide, Air Quality, and Poison

An elderly couple died as a result of carbon monoxide poisoning. It is believed that the hot water heater and the furnace in the house were not properly vented.

A father and his son died on a camping trip from carbon monoxide poisoning after they brought a heater into their tent which released carbon monoxide gas.

 One of the greatest threats to the quality of air within your home is carbon monoxide (CO). It is a subtle yet dangerous threat that is intensified by the fact that the gas is colorless, odorless, and tasteless. Each year, nearly three hundred people in the United States die from carbon monoxide. Thousands of other people probably suffer the effects of this gas without even realizing it.

When Carbon Monoxide Poisoning Risk Is Greatest

The most dangerous time for CO poisoning is during the fall and winter. The symptoms include headaches, dizziness, nausea, irregular breathing, and fatigue. Consequently, many cases of poisoning probably go undetected. If you have any of these symptoms, open all the doors and windows and go outside. If you feel better once you are outside but the symptoms reappear once you go back inside, you could have CO poisoning.

What to Do If You Are Experiencing Carbon Monoxide Poisoning

If you suspect that you are experiencing carbon monoxide poisoning, do the following things:

- ☐ Get fresh air immediately.
- ☐ Open windows and doors for increased ventilation.
- ☐ Turn off any combustion appliances.
- ☐ Leave the house.

If you do nothing, you could die from CO poisoning. Contact a doctor immediately and tell him or her that you suspect carbon monoxide.

Checking Your Home

Certain clues can signify a problem with carbon monoxide. Check to see if you have any of these problems:

- ☐ Rusting or water streaking on vent or chimney
- ☐ Loose or missing furnace panel
- ☐ Sooting
- ☐ Loose or disconnected vent or chimney connections
- ☐ Debris or soot falling from chimney, fireplace, or appliance
- ☐ Loose masonry on chimney or moisture inside of windows

If you have these problems in addition to the aforementioned symptoms, contact a service technician, a medical professional, or a city official such as your fire marshal immediately.

How to Prevent Carbon Monoxide Poisoning

Households can prevent carbon monoxide poisoning by following these tips and purchasing a carbon monoxide detector:

- ☐ Ensure proper functioning of gas ranges, fireplaces, heaters, furnaces, and gas stoves.
- ☐ Install appliances according to the manufacturer's instructions and local building codes.
- ☐ Follow manufacturer's instructions for safe operation of appliances and heat sources.
- ☐ Inspect and service the heating system, including chimneys and vents, annually.
- ☐ Examine chimneys and vents for improper connections, visible rust, or stains.
- ☐ Check for signs of improper appliance operation, such as decreasing hot water supply, furnace running constantly or unable to heat, sooting, or an unfamiliar or burning odor.
- ☐ Never service appliances without proper knowledge, skills, and tools.
- ☐ Never use a gas range or oven for heating or a gas-burning appliance in a closed room.
- ☐ Never burn charcoal indoors or in a garage.
- ☐ Do not run an automobile in a closed garage for even a second.

Purchasing a Carbon Monoxide Detector

Carbon monoxide detectors are devices you install in your home to detect the presence of carbon monoxide. Such a device acts like a smoke detector because it too is an early-warning detection device. You should buy more than one, because it is important to put them on each floor of your home and near the bedrooms, garage door, the kitchen, the furnace, and/or other combustible-heat sources. Carbon monoxide detectors should meet standards set by Underwriter's Laboratories. Some models have been overly sensitive, and have given false alarms. New models are more reliable, and their alarms will sound only if CO levels are actually high. Detectors can be either plugged into electrical outlets or supported by batteries, just like most smoke detectors.

Indoor Air Quality

Indoor air quality is an extremely important issue, and many people fail to recognize poor air quality as a serious health threat. Air quality is affected by many factors, such as asbestos, combustion by-products, tobacco smoke, formaldehyde, lead, organic gases, carpeting, pesticides, and biological elements, such as pollen and dust. Animals also create air pollutants from their dander, hair, feathers, or skin. Poor air quality can lead to tiredness, dizziness, itchy eyes, scratchy throat, asthma attacks, the spread of infectious diseases, and even a heightened risk of cancer. People at risk are the young, the elderly, and the chronically ill. Because people spend a lot of time inside their homes, and because of the multitude of threats to air quality, the air inside your home can pose a more serious health threat than the air outside your home.

Contaminants

Many threats to air quality exist. The most common threats are as follows:

Biological

Biological contaminants include bacteria, mold and mildew, viruses, pollen, animal traces, and insects. Humidity is a major cause for their growth in your home. The accumulation of these contaminants can result in health problems for you and your family.

Combustion Products

Combustion appliances, such as heaters, stoves, and fireplaces, can pollute homes with such contaminants as carbon monoxide and nitrogen dioxide, as well as other particles.

Household Products

Organic chemicals are widely used as ingredients in household products. Many cleaning, disinfecting, and cosmetic products contain and can release organic solvents, which can cause damage to the nervous system and may even cause cancer.

Lead

Lead is very dangerous and has been banned from house paint, cans, and gasoline. The problem of lead is now confined mainly to older homes with older paint and to ceramic products, glassware, and pottery products that are old or that were bought outside of the United States.

Radon

Radon is a colorless and odorless gas that can be found everywhere. It can enter homes through cracks in the walls or floors as well as from well water and other sources. It does not become a problem unless it becomes trapped in your home. Radon has been implicated as a cause of lung cancer.

Indoor Air Quality Checklist: Room-by-Room

One of the best ways to determine the quality of air inside your home is to go from room to room to examine the threats and remedies one by one. Here is what the U.S. Consumer Product Safety Commission recommends:

All Rooms
- ☐ Clean your house and vacuum regularly.
- ☐ Open doors and windows to ventilate home.
- ☐ Maintain moderate temperature and humidity.
- ☐ Use dehumidifiers and exhaust fans to decrease moisture.
- ☐ Do not smoke in your home.
- ☐ Verify that floor tiles do not contain asbestos.
- ☐ Wash bedding in hot water regularly to get rid of house dust mites.
- ☐ Avoid draperies, because they may be treated with a formaldehyde-based finish.

Bathroom
- ☐ Rather than using air fresheners, open a window or use an exhaust fan.
- ☐ If you do use an air freshener, follow the directions.
- ☐ For moisture, mold, and mildew, install and use an exhaust fan.
- ☐ Fix plumbing leaks promptly.
- ☐ Ventilate properly when using personal-care products, for example, hair spray or nail polish.

Bedroom
- ☐ Never accept dry-cleaned goods with a chemical odor until they have been properly dried. If the problem persists, try a different cleaner.
- ☐ Refill a humidifier with clean water daily, and clean according to instructions.
- ☐ If you use moth repellents, particularly with paradichlorobenzene, avoid breathing vapors and store away from living areas.

Carpeting
- ☐ Clean and dry or remove water-damaged carpets promptly.
- ☐ Verify that the fibers in both the carpet and the pad contain only nontoxic glues.
- ☐ Demand adhesives with low emissions, if they are needed at all.
- ☐ When installing new carpet, ask your retailer to air out the carpet before installation.
- ☐ Leave your home during and after installation. Open doors and windows and use window fans or room air conditioners.
- ☐ After installation open all your doors and windows and ventilate your home for seventy-two hours.

Garage
- ☐ Do not idle car in garage.
- ☐ Open windows when using paint. Follow the directions. Buy limited quantities. Reseal containers well and clean brushes and other materials outside your home.
- ☐ Use nonchemical methods of pest control rather than pesticides. Follow directions for proper use. Mix or dilute outdoors. Open windows when using indoors. Take plants or pets outside when applying pesticides. Call the EPA at 1-800-858-PEST for more information.

Kitchen
The primary threat in the kitchen is household cleaners, moisture from cooking and dishwasher use, and unvented gas stoves and ranges.

- ☐ When you use household cleaners, open a window and follow directions.
- ☐ Install and use an exhaust fan to do away with moisture from cooking and dishwashers.

- [ ] To properly use unvented gas stoves and ranges, keep burners adjusted, install and use an exhaust fan, and never use to heat your home.

Living Areas

- [ ] When buying new paneling, pressed-wood furniture, or cabinets, ask whether they contain formaldehyde. Pressed-wood products with polyurethane or laminates may reduce formaldehyde emissions. Open windows after installation and maintain moderate temperature and humidity.

Indoor Air Quality Checklist: By Contaminant

Indoor air quality safety can be improved by following these safety tips, grouped by contaminant, including biological contaminants, combustion products, lead, and radon.

Biological Contaminants

- [ ] The key to decreasing biological contaminants is to reduce moisture.
- [ ] Install and use exhaust fans that are vented to the outside in kitchens and bathrooms.
- [ ] Make sure that clothes dryers are vented outdoors.
- [ ] Ventilate the attic and crawl spaces.
- [ ] Dry and clean water-damaged carpet and building materials within twenty-four hours.
- [ ] Clean house regularly.
- [ ] If using humidifiers, clean water trays and fill with fresh, distilled water daily.

Combustion Products

- [ ] Keep gas appliances properly adjusted.
- [ ] Consider purchasing vented gas space heaters and furnaces.
- [ ] Use proper fuel in kerosene heaters.

☐ Install and use exhaust fans vented to the outside for gas stoves.

☐ Open flues when gas fireplaces are in use.

☐ Choose properly sized wood stoves that are certified to meet EPA emission standards.

☐ Make certain that doors on all wood stoves fit tightly.

☐ Have a trained professional inspect, clean, and tune up your central heating system.

☐ Do not idle your car in the garage.

Lead

☐ Replace items that contain lead, but be careful of creating lead dust.

☐ Have a professional remove lead-based paint.

☐ Leave lead-based paint manufactured before 1978 undisturbed if in good condition.

☐ Contact the state and local health and housing departments to inquire into any possible lead poisoning prevention programs.

Radon

☐ Seal cracks and other openings in the basement floor.

☐ Ventilate crawl spaces.

☐ Install subslab or basement ventilation or air-to-air heat exchangers.

☐ Open windows to reduce the amount of radon without increasing radon exposure.

☐ Do not smoke in your home. Smoking is a major source of radon.

☐ Treat radon-contaminated well water by aerating or filtering through granulated activated charcoal.

Since health is a major concern in everyone's life, ensuring the quality of your air at home will increase your quality of life.

Poisons

A fifteen-year-old boy mistook a highly corrosive, clear electrolyte solution for water because it had been shipped in a reused plastic one-gallon milk container that lacked appropriate warnings. The teenager drank it and died two weeks later from severe internal injuries.

Poisons are substances that, if inhaled, ingested, absorbed, or injected, harm the structures or functions of the body. Some types of poisons may act immediately; other ones may act more slowly. Some poisons, such as cyanide, are so toxic they only require a minute amount to be harmful, while others, such as garden sprays and lead, are cumulative and require exposure over a long period to achieve the same level of toxicity. Many are carcinogenic and cause fatal cancers some years after exposure.

What Are the Types of Poisons?

Iron, mercury in fish, lead, dietary supplements and vitamins, medicine, alcoholic beverages, cologne, perfume, mouthwash, art supplies, cigarette butts, household plants, and many other substances pose risks for poisoning.

Recognizing the Symptoms of Poisoning

The wide varieties of poisonous substances represent a broad range of symptoms. For children, look for the following symptoms:

- ☐ They can't follow you with their eyes.
- ☐ They're sleepy before nap time.
- ☐ Their eyes go around in circles.
- ☐ You find burns around the lips or mouth.

☐ You find stains of the substance around the child's mouth or the smell of the substance on the child's breath.

☐ You find an opened or spilled bottle of pills.

In the case of adults, look for signs such as pale or cool skin, an erratic pulse, nausea and/or vomiting, burns around the mouth, blurred vision, ringing in the ears, smell of fumes or odors, stomach pains or cramps, or drowsiness.

How to Treat a Poisoning Victim

To treat a poisoning victim, take the following steps:

☐ Remain calm.

☐ Call the nearest poison control center or, for medicine poisoning, your physician.

☐ To induce vomiting, experts recommend keeping on hand syrup of ipecac, but don't use it unless you are advised by the physician or poison control to do so. It usually works within a half hour of ingestion. Store ipecac away from children.

☐ For household chemical ingestion, follow first aid instructions on the label, and then call the poison control center or your doctor.

☐ When you call, tell them the victim's age, height, and weight, existing health conditions, as much as you know about the substance involved, the exposure route (swallowed? inhaled? splashed in the eyes?), and if the person has vomited.

☐ If you know what substance the person has ingested, take the remaining solution or bottle with you to the phone when you call.

☐ Follow the instructions of the poison control center precisely.

Preventing Poisonings

Whatever the substance, remember that prevention of a potential problem is essential. Always ensure that poisonous substances are kept away from children and that pills and medications are locked away in a childproof cupboard. Children are attracted to brightly colored items and vitamins made to look like cartoon characters. Substances must never be decanted into attractive containers such as soft drink bottles. All substances must be labeled and understood before use. Prescription medications are to be used only by the person to whom they were prescribed. All poisons and medications should be disposed of correctly.

Tamper-Prevention Techniques

Tampering is a serious concern with medicine and other products that people buy to consume. Since the Tylenol scare in 1982, when capsules laced with cyanide killed seven people, proper packaging to protect the contents and the user from poisoning has been a major concern. To guard against products that may have been tampered with, use the following guidelines.

- ☐ Read the label.
- ☐ Inspect the outer packaging before you buy.
- ☐ Inspect the medicine when you open the package and look again before you take it. If it looks suspicious, be suspicious.
- ☐ Look for capsules or tablets that are different in any way from others in the package.
- ☐ Don't use any medicine from a package with cuts, tears, slices, or other imperfections.
- ☐ Don't take medicine in the dark. Read the label and look at the medicine for each dose.

Poison Lookout Checklist

The U.S. Consumer Product Safety Commission recommends the following to ensure that your children and loved ones are safe from poisons:

Your Kitchen

Do all harmful products in the cabinets have child-resistant caps?

Products like furniture polishes, drain cleaners, and some oven cleaners should have safety packaging to keep little children from accidentally opening them. They also should be stored out of the reach of children.

Are all potentially harmful products in their original containers?

You should always keep products, including any medications, in their original containers. This should be done for two reasons. First, labels on the original containers often give first aid information to use if someone swallows the product. Second, if products are stored in containers like drinking glasses or pop bottles, someone may think they are food, a beverage, or candy and swallow them.

Are harmful products stored away from food?

☐ Do not place harmful products in close proximity to food. If harmful products are placed next to food, someone may accidentally get the food and poisons mixed up and swallow the poison.

☐ Place all potentially harmful products out of the reach of children.

☐ Lock all cabinets that contain dangerous products. The best way to prevent poisoning is to make sure that it's impossible to find and get at the poisons. Locking all cabinets that hold dangerous products is the best poison prevention.

Your Bathroom

Do you remember that medicine could poison if used improperly?

Many children are poisoned each year by overdoses of aspirin. If aspirin can poison, think of how many other poisons might be in your medicine cabinet. Aspirin and most prescription drugs come with child-resistant caps. These caps have been shown to save the lives of children.

- ☐ Make sure that your aspirin and other potentially harmful products have child-resistant closures.
- ☐ Check your prescriptions before leaving the pharmacy to make sure the medicines are in child-resistant packaging.
- ☐ Follow dosage instructions.

Have you thrown out all out-of-date prescriptions?

As medicines get older, the chemicals inside them can change. What was once a good medicine may now be a dangerous poison. Flush all old drugs down the toilet. Rinse the container well and then discard it.

Are all medicines in their original containers with the original labels?

Prescription medicines may not list ingredients. The prescription number on the label will, however, allow rapid identification by the pharmacist of the ingredients, should they not be listed. Without the original label and container, you can't be sure what you're taking. After all, aspirin looks a lot like poisonous roach tablets.

If your vitamins or vitamin/mineral supplements contain iron, are they in child-resistant packaging?

Most people think of vitamins and minerals as foods and, therefore, as nontoxic, but a few iron pills can kill a child.

Your Garage or Storage Area
Did you know that many things in your garage or storage area that can be swallowed are terrible poisons?

Death may occur when people swallow such everyday substances as charcoal lighter, paint thinner and remover, antifreeze, and turpentine.

General Tips
- ☐ Do all these poisons have child-resistant caps?
- ☐ Are they stored in the original containers?
- ☐ Are the original labels on the containers?
- ☐ Have you made sure that no poisons are stored in drinking glasses or pop bottles?
- ☐ Are all these harmful products locked up and out of sight and reach?

For immediate information on a potential poisoning, call the national poison-control center's toll-free number, 1-800-222-1222.

6

Food Safety:
How Safe Is Your Food?

More than fifty people were affected by a listeria outbreak in the northeastern United States. It is thought that the outbreak was caused by contaminated precooked, sliceable turkey deli meat. Since that time, the manufacturer has recalled twenty-seven million pounds of meat.

Before she went to bed, a day-care provider put some chicken into the refrigerator to defrost. She took it out the next morning and cut it up on a wooden cutting board. She then put the chicken back into the refrigerator to marinate until supper. She wiped the cutting board with a sponge before she went to greet her first day-care child. Later that morning she chopped raw vegetables for the children's snacks on the cutting board. Two of the children were vomiting the next day.

We need food to survive, but it can be dangerous if not handled properly. Most people don't give much thought to food safety until a food-borne illness, or food poisoning, happens to them. The problem of food poisoning is exacerbated by the emergence of new food-borne germs and bacteria, the increased virulence and resistance of existing organisms to our immune system, and the greater susceptibility of certain people to food-borne infections. The threats are real, numerous, and varied, as headlines in recent years have documented: E. coli bacteria in meat and apple juice, salmonella in eggs and poultry, pesticides on vegetables, cyclospora on fruit, cryptosporidium in drinking water, and the hepatitis A virus in frozen strawberries. Aside from vomiting or diarrhea, food poisoning can result in serious illness and even death. It can take a lot of the fun out of eating!

Millions of cases of food-borne illness occur annually, especially from meat and poultry products; however, many cases go undetected because many people think they have a virus or the flu instead of a food-borne illness. Food-borne illness costs billions of dollars each year in medical costs and indirect costs. People most at risk include pregnant women, children, the elderly, people with lowered immunity due to HIV/AIDS, people taking antibiotics or antacids, and people taking medication for cancer treatment or organ transplants. Despite high-profile incidents of food-borne illness and food contamination, the U.S. food supply is among the world's safest.

Food Safety Checklist

Examine Food

There are two types of changes in food: quality and safety. Educate yourself about food and become aware of the signs that food is unsafe:

☐ Quality: Browning, drying out, rancidity, dissolving, separation, ice crystal damage in frozen foods. Look at the expiration dates for commercially manufactured foods.

☐ Safety: Bad odors, slime, moldy food; canned foods with bad odors, color, or texture.

If you find any food with any of these characteristics, throw it out immediately.

Keep Hot Foods Hot and Cold Foods Cold

Perishable foods—meats, poultry, fish, cooked vegetables, dairy products, and eggs—that become warm are not safe, because bacteria can grow quickly.

☐ Store foods below 40 degrees Fahrenheit or above 140 degrees Fahrenheit.

☐ Do not consume perishable foods that have been held between 40 and 140 degrees Fahrenheit for more than three hours.

☐ Check barbecue and microwave foods carefully; uneven heating is common.

When You Go to a Buffet Line or Are Serving One

☐ Make sure that plates are hot and that the buffet has chafing dishes and beds of ice.

☐ The restaurant or cafeteria should rotate small amounts of food and should not combine leftover food with fresh food.

Cover and Refrigerate Leftovers Promptly

☐ Set casserole dishes in a pan of cold water for quick cooling. Hot foods that have cooled enough in the bowls so you can pick them up with bare hands may be placed in the refrigerator to cool if bowls are a maximum of three inches deep and jars a maximum size of half a gallon. Larger containers cool too slowly to be safe.

Wash Hands and Work Surfaces Well

- ☐ Wash hands routinely and thoroughly with soap and lots of water.
- ☐ Wash hands again after any interruption or when handling a different type of food.
- ☐ Scrub cutting boards, countertops, and other surfaces with soap and water and rinse with a bleach-water solution after they are exposed to raw meat, fish, or poultry.
- ☐ Check the cleanliness of kitchen utensils such as the can opener and cutting board.
- ☐ Replace plastic boards when scarred.
- ☐ Do not use wooden boards with raw meats, because they are difficult to clean.

Prevent Cross-Contamination

Cross-contamination occurs when an uncooked animal product touches food that is consumed without further cooking.

- ☐ Wash hands carefully and thoroughly before cooking and during food preparation.
- ☐ Do not reuse shopping bags or egg cartons.
- ☐ Refrain from breaking eggs on the edge of a counter, which results in contamination.
- ☐ Do not wash poultry, because this spreads bacteria instead of getting rid of it.
- ☐ Do not put cooked food on the same plate as raw foods, especially for barbecues.
- ☐ Do not use marinades for basting raw meat and poultry.

☐ Boil marinades if they are also to be served with the meat.

☐ Do not use the same cutting board for raw meats and salads.

When You Reheat Leftovers

☐ Refrigerate leftovers and other perishable foods within two hours of cooking.

☐ Heat food until it bubbles to eliminate non-heat-resistant toxins and live microbes.

☐ Be aware that talking over food spreads bacteria, which then may be present in food.

Wash Foods Thoroughly

To guard against pesticides and other chemicals that are used on the U.S. food supply for various purposes, follow these steps:

☐ Always scrub and wash food products thoroughly.

☐ Wash fruit and vegetables with large amounts of cold or warm tap water and scrub with a brush, when appropriate. Do not use soap to clean food products.

☐ Throw away the outer leaves of leafy vegetables such as lettuce and cabbage.

☐ Trim the fat from meat, and fat and skin from poultry and fish.

How to Buy Fresh Fish

Fish spoil easily and harbor various kinds of bacteria. To guard against food poisoning, follow these steps.

☐ The fish's eyes should be clear and bulge a little. Only a few fish, such as walleye, have naturally cloudy eyes.

☐ Whole fish and fillets should have firm and shiny flesh. Dull flesh may mean the fish is old. Fresh whole fish also should have bright red gills, free from slime.

☐ If the fish's flesh does not spring back when pressed, the fish is not fresh.

☐ There should be no darkening around the edges of the fish or brown or yellowish discoloration.

☐ The fish should smell fresh and mild, not fishy or ammonia-like.

Care Labels

☐ Always follow any labels for proper handling, storage instructions, or expiration dates.

☐ Do not confuse these instructions with instructions designed to preserve the quality and prolong the shelf life of nonperishable foods such as salad dressings, packaged puddings, and canned main dishes.

Microwave Ovens

☐ Remove food from store wrap before defrosting or cooking.

☐ Arrange food items uniformly in a covered dish.

☐ Stir or rotate food once or twice during microwaving.

☐ Be careful not to partially cook food.

☐ Cook meat and poultry immediately after defrosting.

☐ Cook large pieces of meat on medium power for longer times.

☐ Debone large pieces of meat.

☐ Do not microwave whole, stuffed poultry.

☐ After microwaving food, use a meat or oven thermometer to ensure food is at a safe temperature.

☐ Use microwave-safe utensils and do not place aluminum

foil, cold storage containers such as margarine tubs, or cheese containers in the microwave oven.

(Source: Food and Drug Administration [FDA])

Cooking and Defrosting

Meat

- ☐ Cook ground beef, veal, lamb, or pork to an internal temperature of 160 degrees Fahrenheit.
- ☐ Cook ground chicken or turkey to an internal temperature of 165 degrees Fahrenheit.
- ☐ Cook whole or pieced chicken to an internal temperature of 180 degrees Fahrenheit.
- ☐ Cook fish fillets and whole fish to an internal temperature of 160 degrees Fahrenheit.

Eggs

- ☐ Eggs should be cooked throughout to 140 degrees Fahrenheit or above.
- ☐ Scrambled eggs should be cooked at least one minute at 250 degrees Fahrenheit.
- ☐ Poached eggs should be cooked for five minutes in boiling water.
- ☐ Sunnyside fried eggs should be cooked in the frying pan at 250 degrees Fahrenheit for the following times:
  - — Uncovered: Fry for at least seven minutes.
  - — Covered: Fry for at least four minutes.
- ☐ Eggs fried "over easy" should be cooked with the frying pan at 250 degrees Fahrenheit for the following times:
  - — Fry for at least three minutes on one side.
  - — Fry for at least two minutes on the other.

☐ Boiled eggs in the shell should be cooked while completely submerged in boiling water for seven minutes.

Defrosting

☐ Defrost foods in the refrigerator, in cold water, or in a microwave oven.

(Sources: FDA and USDA)

7

Holiday Safety: Preparing for the Holidays

A fifty-four-year-old man was found lying on the ground with a large burn hole in one of his pant legs. The man had been on a long metal extension ladder, removing Christmas lights from a large pine tree in front of his home. The lights got entangled on a power line, and the man fell thirty feet to the ground. He died of high-voltage electrocution.

An eight-year-old girl received second- and third-degree burns to her leg when a spark from a sparkler she was holding ignited her dress.

 When holidays approach and families get together, safety is of utmost concern. Many generations come together—children, parents, and grandparents—for the holidays. Few things are worse than a joyous occasion ruined by an accident. Consumers should ensure the safety of their children, older people, their homes, and their holiday preparations.

Independence Day

Fireworks, family, celebration, and recreation are the things that we all enjoy about the Fourth of July. Nothing is like going to the park with thousands of other people and watching a fireworks display, or having a backyard barbecue with your family and friends. It is a great day of relaxation, backyard barbecues, magnificent fireworks displays, and catching up with all the family members. One of the unfortunate characteristics of this day is that injuries also occur. Fireworks, heat, and recreational activities cause most of the injuries suffered on Independence Day.

Fireworks Safety

One of the most traditional yet dangerous ways to celebrate our nation's independence is to set off fireworks, smoke bombs, rockets, Roman candles, and noisemakers bought from fireworks stands. They can be loud, beautiful, and amazing, which is why we all like them so much, but they also can be very dangerous. The U.S. Consumer Product Safety Commission (CPSC) estimates that several thousand people are treated for fireworks-related injuries each Independence Day. Fireworks can cause injuries when they are misused or when they malfunction.

Despite these morbid facts and because of the enactment of rigid safety standards for consumer fireworks, a safe, enjoyable backyard fireworks display is now possible. Although this book recommends that you should stick to backyard barbecues and public fireworks displays, if you do choose to buy fireworks, it is very important to be extremely careful and to follow safety guidelines.

Checklist: Fireworks Safety
- ☐ Always read and follow label directions.
- ☐ Have an adult present.
- ☐ Buy from reliable fireworks sellers.

- ☐ Ignite fireworks outdoors.
- ☐ Have water handy.
- ☐ Never experiment or attempt to make your own fireworks.
- ☐ Light one at a time.
- ☐ Never reignite malfunctioning fireworks.
- ☐ Never give fireworks to small children.
- ☐ Store fireworks in a cool, dry place.
- ☐ Dispose of fireworks properly.
- ☐ Never throw fireworks at another person.
- ☐ Never carry fireworks in your pocket.
- ☐ Never shoot fireworks in metal or glass containers.
- ☐ If your family likes fireworks, plan to watch fireworks displays rather than buying fireworks and detonating them yourself.

(Source: U.S. Consumer Product Safety Commission)

Heat

To beat the heat, be sure to drink plenty of liquids.

Recreational Activities

For recreation such as cookouts and other activities, it is important to follow safe practices. Cookouts present several hazards to look out for.

Outdoor Cookouts

What better and more traditional way to celebrate Independence Day than by having an outdoor cookout. It is a great way to spend the holiday with friends and families, and food off the grill always tastes so good. Yet, with all the good times, hazards may be lurking. The heat of the summer sun and the preparation of the food are two areas where dangers reside. Heat-related illnesses or bouts of food poisoning may spoil your holiday. Follow these tips to prevent such nasty incidents:

☐ Have the grill checked once a year by a professional for leaks.

☐ Buy an electric lighter or briquettes treated with starter fluid when using charcoal grills.

☐ Do not use gasoline, kerosene, or other substances not made to be starter fluids.

☐ Be aware that fuel vapors are heavier than air and tend to concentrate near the ground below grills, so explosions or fires can result.

☐ Be careful with fuel; do not expose to heat or direct sunlight or use in enclosed areas.

☐ Make available plenty of beverages and fans or shade.

☐ Schedule your cookout for later in the day.

☐ Follow food preparation and handling instructions.

Other Recreational Activities

Many families go boating or swimming or play games. These activities are excellent ways to spend the holiday. Exercise normal caution whenever you engage in these activities. (For further information, please see the section on recreational and sports safety in chapter 11.)

Halloween

When the season turns from summer to autumn and the kids go back to school, it is not long before Halloween. This holiday can be fun, special, and memorable. Trick-or-treat is a cherished tradition; yet, in recent years a few people have taken some of the innocence out of it by poisoning and putting needles and other objects in the candy. In addition, when children are around the neighborhood, the chances for accidents increase. Precautions must be taken to ensure that the kids are safe when they are having fun.

Halloween Safety Tips

By following these safety tips, you will ensure that you and your family have a safe and happy Halloween:

Costume Safety
- ☐ Make sure that all costume labels are flame resistant.
- ☐ Minimize the risk of contact with candles and other fire sources.
- ☐ Avoid costumes made with flimsy materials and outfits with big, baggy sleeves or billowing skirts.
- ☐ Choose costumes that are light and bright enough to be visible to motorists.
- ☐ Costumes should be short enough to prevent children from tripping.
- ☐ Children should wear well-fitting, sturdy shoes.
- ☐ Tie hats and scarves securely to keep them from slipping over children's eyes.
- ☐ Apply a natural mask of cosmetics rather than a loose-fitting mask that restricts breathing or obscures vision.
- ☐ If a child wears a mask, make sure it fits securely and has eyeholes large enough to allow full vision.
- ☐ Swords, knives, and similar costume accessories should be of soft and flexible material.
- ☐ Decorate or trim costumes with reflective tape that will glow in car headlights.
- ☐ Ensure that bags or sacks are of light colors or decorated with reflective tape, which you can buy in hardware, bicycle, and sporting goods stores.

For Trick-or-Treaters
- ☐ Carry a flashlight.
- ☐ Walk, don't run.
- ☐ Stay on sidewalks.

- ☐ Obey traffic signals.
- ☐ Stay in your neighborhood.
- ☐ Don't cut across yards or driveways.
- ☐ Make sure costumes don't drag on the ground.
- ☐ Shoes should fit (even if they don't go with your costume).
- ☐ Avoid wearing masks while walking from house to house.
- ☐ Carry only flexible knives, swords, or other props.
- ☐ Walk on sidewalk, or the left side of the road facing traffic if there is not a sidewalk.
- ☐ Wear clothing with reflective markings or tape.
- ☐ Approach only houses that are lit.
- ☐ Go to the homes of people you know.

For Parents
- ☐ Make sure your child eats dinner before setting out.
- ☐ Children should carry a cell phone or carry quarters so that they can call home.
- ☐ Make sure young children are accompanied by an adult or responsible teenager.
- ☐ Instruct children to trick-or-treat in their neighborhood and on well-lighted streets.
- ☐ Give children a flashlight to carry with them.
- ☐ Teach children to walk on sidewalks or the left side of the street facing cars.
- ☐ Know which friends your children are with and which route they are taking.
- ☐ Leave your porch light on so children know it's okay to visit your home.
- ☐ Don't let children eat anything until they are home and the treats are examined.
- ☐ Cut and wash fruit before eating.
- ☐ Set aside anything that looks suspicious and call the police; otherwise, throw away unsealed foods.

- ☐ Inform older children how to reach you and when to be home.
- ☐ Try to replace trick-or-treating on the street with events at school, church, and so forth.

For Homeowners

- ☐ Clear your yard of such things as ladders, hoses, dog leashes, and flower pots.
- ☐ Battery-powered jack-o'-lantern candles are preferable to real ones.
- ☐ If using real candles, place the pumpkin away from where trick-or-treaters will walk.
- ☐ Make sure paper or cloth yard decorations cannot be blown into a flaming candle.
- ☐ Give out healthy food alternatives for trick-or-treaters, such as sealed peanut-butter crackers, single-serving cereal, fruit rolls, or raisins.

For Drivers

- ☐ Drive slowly all evening.
- ☐ Adult Halloween party goers should have a designated driver.

(Source: U.S. Consumer Product Safety Commission)

Thanksgiving

Each year as we prepare our homes for holiday traditions, nostalgia fills the air. My family in the United States always spent the holidays with my Aunt Ethel and Uncle Frank Welles. What a treat it was! Besides the joy of just being together, we always had a sumptuous dinner of a wonderful roasted turkey, mashed potatoes, several salads, my favorite green bean casserole, my not-so-favorite turnips, and much more. Dessert was always pumpkin or mincemeat pie with a scoop of ice cream. Aunt Ethel put special thought and care into every made-from-scratch dish.

As you prepare to gather with friends and family to give thanks for all the year's blessings, be sure to make it a happy and a safe holiday time. With so much time spent in the kitchen, safety starts there.

Ten Tips for Safe Food Preparation

By following the instructions and suggestions below, you can take charge of the safety of your food and make sure that holiday dinners are delicious and healthy.

- ☐ Thoroughly wash your hands with soap and water before and after each food preparation. This prevents cross-contamination of any of the foods.
- ☐ Prepare the turkey very carefully. Wash it thoroughly and cook it thoroughly. If the turkey is frozen, always defrost it in the refrigerator. Do not leave it on the counter. Salmonella is found in over 50 percent of poultry, so you must be careful when you are handling any poultry products.
- ☐ After the turkey is defrosted, wash it thoroughly and dry it with paper towels. Discard the paper towels immediately. Put the turkey immediately into the roasting pan and then place it in the oven to be cooked. Place a meat thermometer in the turkey and cook it to 170 degrees Fahrenheit (77 degrees Celsius).
- ☐ After preparing the turkey for the oven, wash all counter areas and utensils thoroughly so that there is no cross-contamination from the turkey juices.
- ☐ Prepare and bake the stuffing separately from the turkey. Do not stuff the bird with any stuffing, because contamination could take place.

- [ ] Thoroughly wash all fruits and vegetables. Sometimes there are chemical residues on fruits and vegetables that need to be removed.
- [ ] Keep hot foods hot and cold foods cold until you are ready to serve. Remember that warm is not a safe temperature for food, because bacteria can grow very quickly in warm perishable foods. And if you are serving buffet style, do not keep any foods on the buffet for longer than two hours.
- [ ] When it is time to clear the table and store the food, it is best to put the leftovers in small containers. Small containers allow the food to cool down in the refrigerator more quickly, reducing the potential of bacteria growth.
- [ ] If you are purchasing a prepared dinner from your local supermarket or favorite gourmet shop, be sure to refrigerate any foods that are not going to be eaten immediately.
- [ ] If cider is on your menu, be sure to buy only pasteurized cider. Unpasteurized cider could cause a potential food safety problem. If you have unpasteurized cider, be sure to heat it thoroughly before you drink it.

Generational Safety

Don't forget to think about safety for all the different generations coming to your home for the holidays. Seniors and children deserve special consideration.

Seniors

For seniors, it is best to tape down any loose rugs to prevent tripping and falling. In the bathroom, be sure you have safety strips in the bathtub and a portable safety bar in the bathtub so that they will not slip. If they are bringing their prescription drugs into your home, be sure that they have child-resistant closures on them or have a separate cabinet that can be locked so that the younger children cannot get into them.

Children

Be sure to childproof your home for any little ones coming to your festivities. Lock all cabinets that hold medicines or household cleaners. Put safety closures on your electrical outlets. Be sure that any baby equipment is up-to-date and meets the new standards of the U.S. Consumer Product Safety Commission or similar agency in other countries.

Christmas

Family members get to see each other. Relatives remark about how old the kids are getting. Some family members prepare for the Christmas feast in the kitchen. Other family members sit back in their winter clothing in front of the fireplace and watch football on television. Kids run around the house yelling in excitement. Sounds of laughter and joking permeate the household.

All of this fun and chaos does have its downside. For example, kids are running around and their toys might be lying on the floor, which can endanger both the children and older members of the family. The kitchen poses a danger for children. Things in the kitchen, such as the oven, stove, and hot dishes, produce a potentially hazardous environment for children. Also, Christmas trees as well as Christmas lights can pose a risk of fire.

Buying a Gift of Safety

If safety is important to you, buying a gift of safety might be one of the best and most consequential things you could buy for someone. Here are gift ideas for people with safety in mind:

- ☐ Smoke detectors and batteries
- ☐ A good-quality fire extinguisher
- ☐ A flashlight and batteries or light sticks
- ☐ A first aid kit
- ☐ A carbon monoxide detector
- ☐ A mobile phone
- ☐ A second-floor escape ladder
- ☐ "Emergency kit"—energy bars, water, battery radio, flashlight/light sticks, and a first aid kit—packed in a small travel bag
- ☐ This book

Christmas and Holiday Season Safety Tips

Christmas Trees

- ☐ Consider buying an artificial tree.
- ☐ When buying a real tree, ensure that it does not lose needles when tapped on the ground.
- ☐ Purchase a heat sensor alarm that hangs on the tree. The alarm looks like an ornament.
- ☐ Spray a fresh Christmas tree with a fire retardant.
- ☐ Leave the tree outside until ready to decorate.
- ☐ Keep tree away from floor heaters, the fireplace, or other heat sources.
- ☐ Secure the tree with wire to keep it from tipping.
- ☐ Cut one inch off the trunk to help it absorb water.
- ☐ The stand should hold at least one gallon of water. A six-foot tree will use one gallon of water every two days.
- ☐ Mix a commercial preservative with the water.
- ☐ Check the water level every day.
- ☐ Clean the tree stand to improve the tree's water intake: use one capful of bleach to a cup of water.
- ☐ Fasten the lightbulbs securely and point the sockets down to avoid collecting moisture.

- [ ] Never use candles, even on artificial trees.
- [ ] When children are present, fence off the tree.
- [ ] Dispose of the tree properly. Never burn it in the fireplace.

Christmas Lights and Ornaments

- [ ] Use only UL-approved lights and no more than three strands linked together.
- [ ] Use miniature lights that have cool-burning bulbs.
- [ ] Turn off Christmas lights when asleep or if you leave your home.
- [ ] Check cords to be sure they are not frayed but are strongly built.
- [ ] Never use indoor extension cords outside.
- [ ] Use outdoor lights only outside your home.
- [ ] Avoid placing breakable ornaments or ornaments with small detachable parts on the bottom branches of the tree where children and pets can reach them.

Home Safety

- [ ] Install smoke detectors or new batteries in the ones you have and test them.
- [ ] When using candles, place them a safe distance from combustibles.
- [ ] Place candles in sturdy containers. Remember that hot wax burns kids.
- [ ] Extinguish candles before going to bed.
- [ ] Dispose of fireplace ashes in a metal container until cold enough to discard.
- [ ] Have an operable fire extinguisher readily available.
- [ ] Never burn holiday greenery or wrapping paper in the fireplace.

Holidays mean rest, relaxation, fun, family, friends, and gifts. They are fun times when we can forget about our normal day-to-day worries and our obligations and when we can do more of what we want to do. Independence Day, Halloween, and Christmas are great and special times of the year. Other holidays such as Labor Day, Memorial Day, and New Year's Day are other special occasions when we get to break from the routine. In such special times, the last thing we want is for them to be upset by unfortunate incidents. By following the tips mentioned above and preparing things before these days, the possibility for unwanted incidents or other crises can be reduced.

(Source: U.S. Consumer Product Safety Commission)

8

Mail Safety

 With the anthrax attacks of 2001, we all became nervous when doing the simple daily task of checking the mail. Letters sent to U.S. senator Tom Daschle, members of the media, and the offices of American Media in Florida infected many people and killed several people, including some individuals who had very little exposure to infected mail. Despite the concern that these events generated, the U.S. Postal Service is doing everything possible to ensure the safety of its customers, of its employees, and of the mail itself. The public must assist the U.S. Postal Service to accomplish these goals. Here are some of the tips the postal service recommends.

Signs of Suspicious Mail

It is imperative to know what signs should cause you to be suspicious of your mail. They are the following:

- ☐ It's unexpected or from someone you don't know.
- ☐ It's addressed to someone no longer at your address.
- ☐ It's handwritten and has no return address or bears one that you can't confirm is legitimate.

☐ It's lopsided or lumpy in appearance.

☐ It's sealed with excessive amounts of tape.

☐ It's marked with restrictive endorsements such as "Personal" or "Confidential."

☐ It appears to contain a powdery substance.

☐ It's emanating strange odors or appears to be stained.

☐ It shows a city or state on the postmark that doesn't match the return address.

What to Do If You Suspect a Piece of Mail

If you have come across a piece of mail that seems suspicious, take the following actions:

☐ Don't handle a letter or package that you suspect is contaminated.

☐ Don't shake it, bump it, or sniff it.

☐ Wash your hands thoroughly with soap and water.

☐ Notify local enforcement authorities.

What to Do If You Receive an Anthrax Threat

If you have received a piece of mail that makes an anthrax threat, contains unusual substances, or otherwise seems suspicious and potentially dangerous, take the following steps:

☐ Do not handle the mail piece or package suspected of contamination.

☐ Notify the police.

☐ Make sure the suspicious mail is isolated and leave the area.

☐ Ensure that all persons in contact with the mail wash their hands with soap and water.

☐ List all persons who have touched the letter and/or envelope and their contact information.

☐ Place all items worn when in contact with the suspicious mail in plastic, keep them isolated, and make them available for enforcement agents.

☐ As soon as practical, shower with soap and water.

☐ If prescribed medication by medical personnel, take it until otherwise instructed.

☐ Notify the Center for Disease Control Emergency Response at 1-800-311-3435.

Symptoms and Effects of Anthrax

Although there are other potential biological and chemical agents that could be used in various ways to launch attacks against U.S. citizens, anthrax is the one that has actually been used and that can be so dangerous because of how easy it is to disperse. Once a person has been exposed to anthrax, the incubation period is between one and seven days. There are two types of anthrax poisoning: skin and inhalation. The onset of inhalation anthrax is gradual, and possible symptoms might include fever, malaise, fatigue, cough, and mild chest discomfort followed by severe respiratory distress. After two to four days, there would be more severe symptoms, such as breathing difficulty and exhaustion. At this stage, it would most likely be fatal.

Conclusion

Safe, efficient delivery of mail is what we have come to expect from the postal service. We want the mail we receive in our mailbox on our property or at our place of employment to be safe and secure. With recent events, it has become necessary, unfortunately, to be ever vigilant about guarding your safety and that of your loved ones when checking the mail. Be careful and be prepared.

9

CHILD SAFETY: GUIDELINES FOR PREVENTING INCIDENTS

A child, seventeen months, was found hanging between the mattress and ladder of a metal bunk bed at his home.

Another child, twelve months, was found hanging by a pacifier ribbon that got caught on the rail of her crib.

 Parents are the best judges of safety in equipment for their children. Child safety is an ongoing struggle. Parents are a child's greatest deterrent against serious harm. Make every effort possible to ensure your child's safety and enjoyment.

Baby Safety

A majority of serious baby injuries can be prevented easily by being aware of where the dangers are and how to protect your baby from them. Just because baby equipment is labeled for "baby usage" does not mean it is safe.

Baby Furniture and Equipment

A crib seems like the most harmless of places: a "safe haven," a nurturing area of comfort and ease. It is where we lay our children to sleep. Yet, can you believe that a crib could become one of the most dangerous places you can leave your child without your supervision? Never take your child's safety for granted. Imagine the feeling a first-time parent has when he or she learns of the hazards of a crib or stroller, those very items we as parents and consumers have come to expect to be safe and free from serious harm. From the onset of a child's life, products such as high chairs, cribs, strollers, and playpens intended for a child must be carefully selected to ensure safety at every step. Parents, baby-sitters, and all child caretakers need to be aware of the many potential hazards in their environment—hazards occurring through misuse of the products or those involved with products that have not been well designed for use by children. As parents, the responsibility for the safety of our children is our greatest concern.

Cribs

The U.S. Consumer Product Safety Commission (CPSC) has specified the risks and preventable maintenance involved with baby cribs. Each year children die by either strangulation or suffocation because of the hazards associated with baby cribs. Simple preventive maintenance and supervision can allow your child safe and enjoyable use of his or her crib.

When selecting a crib for your baby, be cautious of older, "hand-me-down" cribs, which might not comply with current safety standards. You should not use a crib that does not meet the current safety standards. You should discard old cribs and should never buy a used crib from a garage sale or flea market.

When purchasing a crib, you should look for the following things: No space between the bars on a crib should exceed two and three-eighths inches. If the spacing is too big, or if there are breaks or missing bars, children can slip through the space and become strangled. Parents are encouraged to use a ruler to measure the spacing between the bars on older and even newer cribs. If the space exceeds that recommended by the CPSC, parents are encouraged to weave cloth between the bars to keep the child from falling through the spacing.

Also shown in the report, corner posts on cribs present a potential danger zone for children, especially if the posts have decorative knobs on the ends. The report suggests that the corner posts should not project more than one sixteenth of an inch above the end panel of the crib. Also, the decorative knobs present an entanglement hazard to children who try to climb up or out of the crib. These decorative posts must be as level as possible with the tops of the rails. Parents are encouraged to unscrew the corner posts or saw them off so that they are level with the top of the crib rails. Parents are also encouraged to make sure that there are no cutouts in the foot or headboards that could cause possible head entrapments.

Even the mattress of a crib is a potential hazard if not monitored correctly. Parents should check the mattress to see if it fits snugly against the sides of the crib so that no more than two fingers can fit in the space. As a precautionary measure, parents can place rolled towels between the mattress and the sides of the crib and check them each time the child is laid in the crib. The report also suggests that the mattress should be covered with a waterproof pad, not by any other form of covering, such as plastic bags or garbage bags. Children cannot breathe if they accidentally get a plastic bag over their nose or mouth.

Not only are the cribs themselves a hazard, but so are the elements around or in a baby crib. Parents are warned to remove bumpers, toys, and mobiles from a crib as soon as a child can push up onto their hands and knees. Children, curious as they are, will use anything they can to help them climb out of a crib. Once a child is up above the crib, they are subject to potential danger, including falling from the crib.

When a child reaches thirty-five inches in height or can climb and/or fall over the sides, the crib should be replaced with a bed. The commission also recommends that the crib not be placed near draperies or blinds. A child could become entangled in or strangled by the cords of these.

As far as general maintenance on the crib, parents should tighten all bolts, nuts, and screws periodically. Whenever the crib is moved, parents are encouraged to be sure that all mattress support hangers are secure. Hooks need to be checked regularly to be sure none are bent or broken. Open hooks may allow the mattress to fall.

High Chairs

A child in a high chair requires constant attention and supervision. If your experience is anything like mine was, you are quite aware of the labors involved at feeding time. Within an instant a child can slip and fall out of the high chair if not properly buckled in. An unstable high chair can tip over.

Parents are encouraged to make sure that any safety belts or straps on the high chair are securely fastened and that the tray is properly secured. Parents are cautioned not to let a child stand up while in the chair and also not to allow other children to climb on the chair. As another safety measure, make sure that the high chair is out of the way of "high-traffic lanes," areas in the home including doorways and paths to the refrigerator or stove. Keeping the high chair far away from tables and walls will keep a child from accidentally pushing it over.

As with any other child equipment, parents should never leave a child unattended in the high chair. Parents are reminded to always use the safety crotch strap, the buckle waist strap, and any other safety straps. Remember that the tray is not a safety restraint but must always be securely fastened. In selecting a suitable high chair, look for those that have a wide and stable base. Any caps or plugs on tubing should be firmly attached so they cannot be pulled off by the child and choked on. Remember that an unattended child can slide beneath the tray if the restraining straps are not used, causing entrapment injuries including strangulation.

Playpens

As harmless as they seem, a playpen is another area of possible danger for children. The styles of playpens that have a drop-side mesh and the ones that are portable mesh cribs, used with a side left down, can pose a serious hazard to newborn babies and infants. When the side is down, the mesh forms a loose pocket into which an infant can fall or roll and suffocate. Drop sides should always be up and locked securely in position when a child is in the playpen. As with a crib, parents are warned not to put in any toys the child can climb on to get out of the playpen. Hinges provide another area of caution. Children seem to have a tendency to get caught in the hinge, causing pinched fingers.

When selecting a playpen, try to choose one that has a small weave of mesh, preferably less than quarter-inch openings. If using a used or handed-down playpen, always inspect the mesh for tears, holes, or loose threads. Also, if using a wooden playpen, make certain that it has slats spaced no more than two and three-eighths inches apart. Also, if staples are used in the construction, inspect them to ensure they are firmly installed and that none are missing or loose.

Strollers and Carriages

When selecting a stroller, look for one that has a wide wheelbase to help prevent tipping. Also, seat belts and crotch straps should be checked to make sure they are securely attached to the frame. Parents should also make sure that the seat belt buckle is easy to fasten and unfasten, so that they will be sure to use it properly each time. Brakes must securely lock the wheels to prevent the stroller from unexpected rolling. Never leave a child unattended in a stroller, because the child may slip into a leg opening, become entrapped by his or her head, and suffer possible strangulation. Just a small amount of common sense could mean the difference between life and death.

Walkers

More children are injured with baby walkers than with any other nursery product, and most serious injuries have occurred when the walkers fell down stairs. New walkers that meet the standards of the Juvenile Products Manufacturers Association (JPMA) are now available, according to the CPSC. Each walker meeting the new standard and certified by the JPMA must meet one of two requirements: Walkers must be too wide to fit through standard door openings, or must have features, such as a gripping mechanism, that will stop the walker at the edge of a stair.

Consumers should replace older walkers with new-generation models that carry the "meets new safety standard" label. Wheeled baby walkers should include features to prevent falls down stairs. Another alternative is the stationary activity center, or saucer, without wheels.

Never accept hand-me-downs or "yard sale" walkers that do not meet the new standards. When using a walker or activity center, close doors or gates at the tops of stairs; keep children within view; keep children away from hot surfaces and containers; move dangling appliance cords, and keep children away from toilets, swimming pools, and other sources of water. For more information, see <http://www.cpsc.gov www.cpsc.gov.> Search on "baby walkers."

Other Furniture

Bassinets and Cradles
- [ ] A bassinet or cradle should have a wide base and be sturdy and stable.
- [ ] Do not use a basket not intended to be a bassinet. Loose wicker can poke and hurt a baby.

Infant Seats (also called bouncer seats)
- [ ] Look for a wide base, nonskid bottom, and a crotch and waist safety belt.

☐ Don't place your baby in an infant seat on top of a counter or table.

☐ Never use an infant seat as a car seat.

Changing Table

☐ Look for a table that is sturdily built, with high sides and a safety strap. Always keep the baby fastened and never turn your back, even for a second.

☐ Keep diaper-changing supplies out of baby's reach.

☐ If you keep a diaper pail near the changing table, be sure it has a locking lid. If it does not, keep it where your child cannot get at it.

Infant Swings

☐ Never leave your baby unattended in either an infant seat or an infant swing.

☐ Use a head support for infants.

☐ The two most common types of injuries from swings are entrapment of a baby's head, when it gets caught between the edge of the backrest and the bars from which the seat hangs, and a backwards fall, when the back of the seat collapses.

Baby-Proofing Your House

Although no child can be completely safe from harm, an informed parent and consumer is the best defense against accidental injury or death. The following section provided by the U.S. Consumer Product Safety Commission consists of a comprehensive checklist to baby-proof your home room by room.

The Nursery

The nursery is very important because it is where your baby will spend most of his or her time; therefore, you should thoroughly examine every inch of this room to ensure that no dangers are present. It is particularly important to make sure the following conditions exist:

- ☐ If the nursery is painted, the paint should be lead free.
- ☐ All baby furniture should be sturdy.
- ☐ Strollers, high chairs, and walkers or saucers should have a nontip design and safety restraint straps.
- ☐ All furniture should have smooth edges and rounded corners.
- ☐ Avoid furniture and other items with rough edges, sharp points, small parts, hinges, and exposed strings, cords, or ribbons.

The Kitchen

The kitchen offers many challenges for the safety-conscious parent. There are many possibilities for disaster located here. Be careful of hot liquids, hot appliances, slippery floors, electrocution risks, sharp objects, poisonous chemicals, and objects your baby can choke on. It may seem that the best way to childproof the kitchen is to put a safety gate at the door. I know that this probably is not possible. What is possible is to make sure that your small child is never left unsupervised in the kitchen.

General Kitchen Safety

- ☐ Keep all cleaning products, pesticides, and other volatile substances locked up.
- ☐ Use unbreakable dishes for feeding a young child.
- ☐ Keep step stools out of reach.
- ☐ Clean up spills immediately to prevent slips and falls.

☐ Keep boxes of plastic kitchen wrap and plastic grocery bags out of your child's reach to avoid suffocation.

☐ Don't use long phone cords that a child could trip on or wrap around his or her neck.

Appliances

☐ Turn the handles of pots and pans toward the back of the stove or counter. Use the back burners for cooking whenever possible.

☐ Don't let your baby play at your feet while you are cooking.

☐ Use a stove guard to prevent your baby from reaching the stove burners.

☐ If your baby can reach the controls on the front of the stove, try installing stove knob covers that the baby can't use.

☐ Never leave a boiling pot or sizzling skillet unattended on the stove.

☐ Teach your child that the oven is "hot" and not to touch.

☐ Install a latch on appliances such as the microwave, refrigerator, and dishwasher.

☐ Keep the dishwasher door closed when not in use. There are many sharp edges inside that can hurt a young child.

☐ Keep plug-in appliances, such as toasters and can openers, high so that your baby can't reach them. Children can get electrocuted if they attempt to plug them in.

Countertops, Cupboards, and Drawers

☐ Never set your baby on a countertop; he or she could fall or reach for harmful items.

☐ Use cabinet and drawer guard latches to keep certain reachable cupboard doors and drawers off-limits to your baby.

☐ Use cord shorteners on appliance cords to keep them away from the baby.

☐ Set aside at least one cabinet for your little one to explore and play with. Store safe items such as Tupperware and nonbreakable pots and pans there.

☐ Keep garbage in a tightly covered container or behind a securely latched cabinet door.

High Chair Safety

☐ Be sure the tray is locked and always secure the restraint system.

☐ To prevent pinching, watch the baby's fingers and hands as you slide the tray on.

☐ Never leave your baby alone in a room in a high chair.

☐ Keep the high chair a safe distance from tables and countertops. A child can tip it over by pushing off with hands and feet.

☐ Make sure your high chair has the JPMA (Juvenile Product Manufacturers Association) label.

The Bathroom

The bathroom can be just as dangerous for your baby as the kitchen is. The combination of water and intriguing appliances can be fascinating to a curious child. Take extra care around this room to protect your little one.

Furnishings

☐ Keep the toilet lid down at all times. If at all possible, place a guard on the lid to lock it.

☐ Place adhesive nonslip stickers in the bathtub and shower to prevent falls.

☐ Use soft, inflated spout covers to save baby from bumps and bruises.

☐ Keep the water temperature set at about 120 degrees Fahrenheit to prevent scalds.

☐ Never, under any circumstances, leave children under five in a tub by themselves.

Medications

☐ All medications should be kept in a locked and very secure place at all times. Remember that a high place is not always a secure place and that medications should be kept out of sight and out of reach.

☐ Make sure all medicines are in child-resistant containers.

☐ Don't save old prescription medicines. Flush them down the toilet when you are finished using them.

☐ Don't tell your child that medicine tastes "like candy" or tastes good. It's better to have to struggle to get them to take it than to tempt them.

☐ Store children's vitamins in a safe place also. Overdosing on vitamins ranks among the top categories of phone calls received by poison control centers.

☐ If your child does manage to swallow or eat any medicine, get whatever you can out of the mouth and call your poison control center or 911 immediately. Keep the poison control center phone number on hand by every phone in your household in case of an emergency such as this.

The Other Rooms of Your Home

As you tour the rest of your home to baby-proof it, you should be on the lookout for the following things:

Doors

☐ Put decals on sliding glass doors so your child won't run into them.

☐ Buy a special guard to keep a patio door locked to prevent your child from opening it and slipping out.

☐ Watch for little fingers when closing doors.

☐ Use doorknob covers on doors you don't want your child

to open. Attach a bell to the door so you can hear it when it does open.

☐ Be aware that any door—front door, bathroom door, basement door—can pose a hazard. Keep them closed.

Electricity

☐ Cover all electrical outlets that are not in use with safety plugs that snap into outlets.

☐ Check behind furniture for exposed outlets that you may have overlooked.

☐ Keep fans up high, out of baby's reach.

☐ Do not use extension cords unless absolutely necessary.

☐ Shorten all cords with cord shorteners.

Furniture and Accessories

The safety of your furniture also should be a concern; furthermore, it is important to stress the need to use caution if you use antique, secondhand, or hand-me-down children's furniture. The best advice is to only use new furniture for youngsters. Although providing your child with the same bed his or her parent or grandparent may have used can be a meaningful and special tradition, it could be very dangerous. If you do use old furniture, inspect the products very carefully on a regular basis.

☐ Put away any unstable or rickety furniture your baby could pull over. Fasten to the wall high bookcases or other tall pieces your child might be able to pull down.

☐ Keep all drawers firmly closed so your baby can't shut fingers in them or climb on them.

Halls and Stairways

☐ Install a safety gate at the top of the stairway.

☐ Place the safety gate's bar latch on the side farthest from your child's reach.

☐ Never leave anything on the stairs you can trip on while carrying your baby.

Windows

☐ Install window guards or adjust windows so they cannot open more than six inches.

☐ Tie up cords to blinds or draperies so that baby can't get entangled in them. Do not place a crib, playpen, high chair, or bed anywhere near these cords.

☐ Install safety glass in large windows and French doors so they won't shatter.

☐ Don't leave furniture or anything else that can be climbed on near a window.

Child Safety

Our children are the most precious possessions we have. Children are also one of the most valuable resources of our country. When we are old, they will be running our country and managing its place in the world. While cars, jewelry, houses, and vacations are valuable and expensive, much more value should be attached to each child's life. One of the most grievous tragedies is when a young one is injured, maimed, or fatally hurt as a result of his or her surroundings or objects of attention. The safety of children is the top priority and the most important safety concern.

Injuries can occur everywhere, and it is a difficult task for parents to ensure that their children are free from all hazards. The key to safety is prevention. For general child safety tips, read below.

Child Safety Checklist

Many things that seem harmless can be dangerous. The U.S. Consumer Product Safety Commission recommends the following guidelines for childproofing your home:

Tips for Parents

- [ ] Never leave children unattended.
- [ ] Medicines, household cleaners, chemicals, or firearms should be kept in locked cabinets, moved to higher shelving, or stored outside the home.
- [ ] All medicine containers should have child-resistant closures.
- [ ] Post emergency phone numbers in plain view and inform everyone where they are.
- [ ] If there are children in your home, all electrical outlets should be capped with plastic plugs.
- [ ] Stairways should be gated with mesh gates, but avoid accordion-style gates.
- [ ] Plastic bags, especially from grocery shopping, should be discarded and kept away from children.
- [ ] Keep pot handles turned toward the rear of the stove.
- [ ] Keep a close eye on children in the kitchen, especially when using stoves and ovens.
- [ ] Take steps to safeguard children from sharp edges on furniture.
- [ ] Store buckets in places inaccessible to children. When not in use, pour out contents.
- [ ] Avoid products with strings, such as Venetian blinds, miniblinds, and clothing with strings over seven inches.
- [ ] Be aware that telephone cords, lamp cords, cords on sacks, and gift-wrapping paper can pose a strangulation and suffocation risk.
- [ ] Keep your household picked up and uncluttered and keep objects off the floor.
- [ ] Do not buy furniture at flea markets, garage sales, or dollar stores.
- [ ] Buy wooden bunk beds, which are safer than other types.

☐ Examine wooden bunk beds for splinters and make sure that guardrails are strong.

Tips for Children

Parents should make sure that their children know the following tips to ensure their own safety:

☐ Don't use alcohol and drugs.
☐ Always go straight to school and directly home from school.
☐ Walk with classmates whenever possible.
☐ If someone tries to touch or hurt you or make you do something you know is wrong, tell your parents or another adult such as a police officer or teacher.
☐ Don't talk to or go with strangers. If you do not know the person, do not go anywhere with him or her.
☐ Never open the door for strangers.
☐ Don't let strangers know if you are home by yourself.
☐ Don't join secret clubs.
☐ Always tell your parents or guardian where you are playing.
☐ Play in safe places such as backyards and playgrounds.
☐ Never play in vacant buildings or construction areas.
☐ Respect other people's property.
☐ Don't let other kids talk you into ruining property or taking things that don't belong to you.
☐ Obey the law.
☐ Ask an adult to help you mark your belongings with an engraver or marking pen.

Toy Safety

An estimated 191,000 people with toy-related injuries were treated in U.S. hospital emergency rooms in 2000.

A two-and-a-half-year-old boy died after riding a foot-propelled toy car into a backyard swimming pool.

Toys are magic to children. When a child receives a toy that was on his or her wish list, the youngster is transported into another world. The toy is more than an object of plastic or metal. It becomes the means by which a little mind's fantasy world is made complete. Even as adults, we may feel tinges of nostalgia if we walk down the toy aisle of a department store. We may long to go back to the time in our lives when toys were magic and allowed us to act our fantasies and dreams.

Because of the special emotions that are brought to them, toys are apart from other products. Children place their trust in the toys that their parents and relatives purchase for them. Little else is as sacred as the innocent trust of a child, and nothing is more tragic than a toy causing an injury or even death to a child. If a toy hurts a child, it is a betrayal that will stay in the minds of a family for many years. Toys are our friends; they are not supposed to hurt us, and it is unforgivable when they do.

Toys are not just playthings. They are also tools for mental, physical, and social growth. We like to find toys that do all of these things; we should not have to worry about their safety. While toys must cater to a child's imagination and creativity, they must be checked to be sure they will not cause danger, accident, injury, or serious harm.

Parents, in the end, are the ultimate safeguards against serious injury to our children. Research shows that the most creative children are those who have had adults involved in their play. The best play happens when the adult takes an active role and plays alongside the child, rather than just providing the toys or supervising the activity. Being a part of your child's play and safety takes practice, yet it is proven to be essential. Our children and the safety of the environment around them are that precious.

What You Can Do to Ensure Safety When Buying Toys

Parents must take time to carefully select a toy before purchasing it and allowing a child to use it in play. When choosing a toy for a child, the following points should be considered:

☐ Is the toy appealing and interesting to the child? All parents are familiar with the toys that never get used, or those that initially were interesting to your child but quickly lost favor.

☐ Parents must ask themselves whether a particular toy is suited for their child's physical capabilities. Not all children progress physically at the same pace, with some being more advanced than others. Parents should make an honest evaluation of their child's physical abilities and purchase toys that are challenging and exciting, yet not overly demanding.

☐ Parents need to be conscientious when purchasing toys, selecting ones that are best suited to the child's mental and social development. Not all children progress at the same level. Remember that the age label has been thoughtfully designed based on many factors, including safety. If you give a child a toy that is too simple or too advanced, he or she may become frustrated and/or become exposed to a safety hazard.

☐ Parents should look carefully for toys that are well constructed, durable, and safe for that child's age group. Parents need to check that all directions and instructions are clear not only to them, but also to the child.

☐ Always read the labels, paying close attention to the recommended age. Parents should look for toys with labels that include words such as "flame retardant" or "flame resistant."

Maintaining Toys

The old cliché "a parent's job is never finished" could not be more appropriate when supervising children and monitoring toys and toy safety. Parents and others responsible for a child's care must become safety experts. Remember, too, that youngsters learn safe habits and responsibility from grown-ups. Parents are encouraged to spot-check toys regularly for minor damage and urge children to let adults know when toys need repair. A damaged or dangerous toy should be immediately repaired, if possible, or discarded. A child does not always see significance in a small crack or tear if a toy is still in one piece. Often a spot of glue, a tightened bolt, or a bit of tape would prevent further damage and a possible accident.

All toys intended for children under eight years old should be free of sharp metal and glass edges. Older toys, through normal use, may break, exposing rough edges. Although the laws ban small parts in the production of new toys for children under three, normal wear and tear can cause small pieces to break from most toys. These parts are small enough to be swallowed or to become lodged in a child's throat, ears, or nose. Parents should pay extra close attention to eyes and noses on stuffed toys and dolls.

Parents are warned not to allow toys to remain outdoors overnight. Rain, snow, and dew cause rust. This is damage that only increases the risk of accidents. Toys must be used, maintained, and stored correctly to ensure that the safety built in at the factory continues in the home. Since toys are among the first things a child considers his or her own, adults should encourage a youngster to assume responsibility by demonstrating how to use and care for toys. Children tend to remember lessons they learn while having fun, so as parents we need to set good examples for proper use and maintenance of toys.

Other Tips

- ☐ Put away toys meant for older children.
- ☐ Be extremely vigilant to keep balloons, marbles, small balls, products with sharp edges or sharp points, paper

clips, rubber bands, and so forth out of the reach of children under three.

☐ Toy chests can strangle, suffocate, or injure children if they do not have proper hinges. Buy a lid support device that will keep the lid from closing all the way.

Playground Safety

A young girl in Louisiana was paralyzed after falling onto a hard playground surface and hitting an exposed concrete footing.

A Michigan child died when the drawstring on her coat hood became entangled in the apparatus of a slide.

It is recess time at any elementary school. Playgrounds across the nation are filled with the sounds of children running and jumping, climbing and exploring. Youngsters are busy speeding down the slides, flying through the air on the swings, and learning balance and motion from a seesaw. This is an important time, a time for children to let their energy loose and to allow their creativity to flow freely.

Yet many times children can do the unexpected on playground equipment, often not performing the activity for which the equipment was originally designed. As curious as they are, children are not always aware of the dangers and risks associated with playground equipment. Sometimes standing on the swing as it soars through the air is more exciting and dangerous than just sitting in one. Yet a child is mostly unaware of the dangers involved. All of this leads to the threat of possible injury or harm.

Children will always want to expand and explore the possibilities that playground equipment presents, and this is not always a negative instinct. The problem only occurs when the risks that children take on could cause serious injury or possibly death. Although there is much effort that goes into making playground equipment safe, it is never injury free. No child is safe from the hazards and risks that are associated with a swing, slide, or seesaw. Yet, being an informed and alert parent could make a significant difference, possibly between life and death.

The Playground: The Basics

Playgrounds are found at parks, schools, child-care facilities, institutions, hotels, restaurants, and resorts. This does not refer to amusement park equipment, or equipment used for sports activities. Because of the numerous possibilities for injury, parents and other adults should always supervise their children while they play in a playground.

A playground should allow children to develop and test their skills by providing challenges; however, these challenges should be appropriate for age-related abilities. Children differ dramatically not only in physical size and ability, but also in their cognitive and social skills. Age-appropriate playground designs should accommodate these differences with regard to the type, scale, and layout of equipment.

Playground Layout

While a playground caters to a broad range of ages, most playground equipment manufacturers and people responsible for the layouts have separated the areas for younger children with equipment of the appropriate size and material to serve children of different abilities. Because supervision is important, the design and scale of equipment should make the age of the intended users obvious. Some playgrounds, often referred to as "tot-lots," are designed only for younger children, so separation is not an issue.

In playgrounds intended to serve children of all ages, the layout of pathways and the landscaping of the playground are specifically designed to create two distinct areas for the two age groups. The areas are usually separated by a buffer zone, an area of ample physical space. Signs in the playground area can be used to give adults a sense of guidance as to the appropriateness of the equipment.

Surfacing

The surfacing of a playground is very important for ensuring the area is safe. Surfacing is a major factor in the prevalence of injuries caused by falls. Obviously, a cement surface is more dangerous than others. When more shock-absorbing materials are used, the number of injuries and deaths sharply declines. The safest and most commonly used materials include mulch, wood chips, sand, gravel, and such substances as rubber matting materials. The surface should be checked frequently and kept as clean as possible from dangers such as broken glass.

General Hazards

Many hazards exist on the playground. Parents should scrutinize the area with the following points to ensure that it meets the standards of the CPSC. First, if your children visit a particular playground often, you should inspect the area frequently to ensure that it continues to be safe. This vigilance is necessary to prevent injuries caused by the development of sharp points or corners resulting from wear on the equipment. While inspecting look out for the following things:

☐ Look for sharp points, corners, or edges on any pieces of playground equipment that could cut or puncture a child's skin. All corners, whether wood or metal, should be rounded. Metal edges should be rolled or have rounded capping; furthermore, you should inspect the slide for sharp edges.

☐ Be aware that the exit end of a slide is a potential danger zone, so always watch your children carefully while they are playing on playground equipment.

☐ Wood parts should be smooth and free from splinters.

☐ Playground equipment should not form openings that could entrap a child's head if the child attempts to enter an opening either feet or head first. An opening may be dangerous if the distance between the interior opposing surfaces is greater than three and a half inches and less than nine inches wide.

☐ Cables, wires, or ropes are serious hazards to running children. Parents should suggest to the proper authorities that such equipment should be brightly colored to guard against injuries caused by running.

☐ Parents should check all anchoring devices on playground equipment to make sure playground equipment will not become dangerously unstable.

☐ Search for rocks, roots, and other protrusions from the ground and either pick up the rocks or restrict the area in which your children can play.

☐ All handrails, ladders, and steps should be properly secured and easily accessible.

Specific Concerns about Equipment

In addition to these general points, there are safety tips appropriate for specific pieces of equipment. Safety on the equipment is just as important as safety around the equipment. One potential danger is the risk of possible strangulation. Clothing strings, loose clothing, and stringed items placed around a child's neck can catch on playground equipment, especially slides and swings.

☐ Parents should avoid dressing their children in loose clothing or clothing with strings.

☐ Hot metal surfaces on playground equipment also are a serious danger. Parents should check the surfaces on the equipment before allowing young children to play on it. Solid steel decks, slides, or steps in direct sunlight may reach temperatures high enough to cause serious burn injuries in a matter of seconds.

☐ Check playground cargo nets before allowing children to climb on them. Some cargo nets have openings with a perimeter length of between seventeen and twenty-eight inches, which could allow a child's head to become entrapped.

Clothing Safety

Clothing protects us against the elements. It keeps us warm in winter and protects us during the summer. The fact that clothing is so necessary requires that it should be harmless, yet sometimes it is not. Most serious hazards can fall into three primary categories: flammability, strangulation, and choking.

Flammability

One of the greatest dangers with clothing is flammability. Often a flammable garment can burn faster than newsprint. Garments made from synthetic fleece fabric are particularly flammable.

Drawstrings

The other most common danger is strings on garments, which could strangle youngsters. Many deaths and injuries are caused each year by drawstring entanglement. Jackets and shirts with hoods represent significant hazards. Drawstrings have gotten caught in playground slides, school buses, cribs, escalators, fences, farm grinders, turn-signal levers, ski chair lifts, and tricycles.

Clothing with Buttons

Clothing with buttons can pose a choking hazard, so for clothing with buttons, test how firmly they are attached to the garment by pulling and yanking the buttons. If any one of them is loose, a youngster may be able to pull the button off; therefore, resew the button, take off the button, or throw away that item of clothing.

Clothing Safety Tips

To ensure that the clothing that your children wear is safe, follow these steps.

- ☐ Ensure that clothing fits properly. Clothing that is too long or too loose may cause tripping or get caught in machinery or open flames.
- ☐ Ensure that buttons and decorative items are fastened securely to the garment.
- ☐ Remove drawstrings from the hoods, waists, and bottoms of children's jackets and other garments.
- ☐ Tuck the ends of scarves into children's jackets.
- ☐ Do not let children wear long scarves, because they pose a strangulation risk.
- ☐ Tie shoelaces properly or buy shoes with Velcro fasteners.
- ☐ If a shoe comes untied, tie it again immediately.
- ☐ Make sure that the seams in socks and mittens do not have loose threads that can wrap around fingers or toes and cut off circulation.
- ☐ Be careful on playgrounds, escalators, and other places where clothing can get caught.
- ☐ Never buy clothing at garage sales, thrift shops, or second-hand shops.
- ☐ Never dress children in hand-me-down clothing, as it may not meet current standards.

10

SENIOR SAFETY: SAFETY CONCERNS FOR SENIORS

On average a third of people age sixty-five and over will fall at least once each year. Half of those age eighty and older will fall at least once a year.

 Safety is important for older consumers. Individuals blessed with a long life should be able to enjoy themselves rather than worry continually about their personal safety. Unfortunately, accidents do occur. Many of these injuries result from hazards that are easy to overlook but that also are easy to fix. By spotting these hazards and taking some simple steps to correct them, many injuries might be prevented.

Safety for the Older Consumer

The U.S. Consumer Product Safety Commission has published a useful checklist to help ensure the safety of older consumers. Act on the following tips to ensure a safer home.

Burns and Fires

- ☐ Remove sources of heat or flame from areas around beds.
- ☐ Never smoke in bed.
- ☐ Use electric blankets according to the manufacturer's instructions.
- ☐ Make sure that nothing is covering an electric blanket when in use. This suggestion includes other blankets, comforters, and pets sleeping on top of the blanket.
- ☐ Avoid tucking in your electric blankets or placing additional coverings on top of them, which can build up excessive heat that can start a fire.
- ☐ Turn off your heating pad before going to sleep. Sleeping with a heating pad on can cause serious burns even at relatively low settings.
- ☐ Install a telephone close to your bed that you can reach without getting out of bed.

Grab Bars

- ☐ Install grab bars in your showers and bathtubs to prevent falls.
- ☐ Attach grab bars, through the tile, to structural supports in the wall, or install bars specifically designed to attach to the sides of the bathtub. Get help to install these, if necessary.
- ☐ Check existing bars for strength and stability. Repair, if necessary.

Medications

- ☐ Make sure that all medicines are stored in proper containers.
- ☐ Be sure that all containers are clearly marked with the

contents, doctor's instructions, the expiration date, and the patient's name.
- [ ] Reclose child-resistant caps tightly.
- [ ] Keep medicine out of the reach of children or locked up in a cabinet.
- [ ] Always use child-resistant closures.
- [ ] Dispose of outdated medicines by flushing pills down the toilet.
- [ ] Pour liquids down the drain and rinse the bottom of the container.
- [ ] Never put medicine in the trash, because young children can take it out.

Rugs and Mats

- [ ] Remove rugs and runners that tend to slide, or apply double-faced adhesive carpet tape or rubber matting to the backs of rugs and runners.
- [ ] Purchase rugs with slip-resistant backing.
- [ ] Check rugs and mats periodically to see if backing needs to be replaced.

Slip Prevention

- [ ] Check bathtubs and showers for nonskid mats, abrasive strips, or nonslip surfaces.
- [ ] Place nonslip mat on bathroom floors.
- [ ] If you are unsteady on your feet, use a stool with nonskid tips while bathing.

Telephone Area

- [ ] Post emergency numbers on or near the telephone. In case of emergency, telephone numbers for the police, fire department, and local poison control center, along with a neighbor's number, should be readily available.

☐ Write the numbers in large print and tape them to the phone, or place them near the phone where they can be seen easily.

☐ If you are elderly, make sure you have access to a telephone in case you fall or have some other accident or emergency.

Water Temperatures

☐ Lower the setting on your hot water heater to "low," or to 120 degrees Fahrenheit. If unfamiliar with your water heater, ask a qualified person to adjust it for you.

☐ Always check water temperature by hand before entering your bathtub or shower, or have a qualified person install a temperature-limiting device on faucets.

☐ For some people it is better to take baths rather than showers to reduce the risk of scalding.

11

OUTDOOR SAFETY: BEING SAFE WHILE HAVING FUN OUTDOORS

A ten-year-old boy was in a hot tub when his arm became stuck in a drain. After being underwater for an undetermined amount of time, he was discovered unconscious and was freed from the drain. He died four days later.

In Dallas, a girl, only ten years old, died of injuries she suffered when a van struck the bicycle she was riding toward an ice cream truck.

Each year about six hundred fires and explosions occur with gas grills, resulting in injuries to about thirty people.

Since 1979 the Consumer Product Safety Commission has received reports of twenty-four deaths from soccer-goal tip-over.

Backyard Safety

 The great outdoors! After working, going to school, or running errands all day, many people love to rest, relax, unwind, play outdoors, and take part in recreational activities. The outdoors offers many opportunities for such activities as swimming, tennis, and barbecues. Yet, many safety dangers lurk outside your home, even in your own backyard.

Your backyard should be childproofed in the same manner as the rest of your house, and there is the potential for many hazards. Even in the most ideal situation, a fenced yard with a minimum of dangers, children should not play alone. Here are some suggestions for what to watch for to prevent potential accidents.

- ☐ Never let an infant or toddler play alone outside.
- ☐ Keep swimming or wading pools inaccessible to babies and toddlers.
- ☐ Check play areas frequently, watching for broken sidewalks that need repair, loose boards on wooden steps, or holes or ditches in the lawn that should be filled.
- ☐ Clean areas of all animal droppings.
- ☐ Watch for poisonous plants such as poison ivy, poison sumac, and poison oak in the backyard, and remove mushrooms and toadstools as soon as they appear.
- ☐ Install childproof locks on gates and remove anything that a child could use to climb.
- ☐ Keep a constant eye on infants who still put objects in their mouths.
- ☐ Make sure outdoor play equipment is safe and sturdily constructed.
- ☐ Place play equipment at least six feet away from fences and walls.

☐ Teach your toddlers or infants about the dangers in their play area.

☐ Create a vocabulary of warning words (*ouch, hot, sharp,* and so forth).

☐ Keep your child out of the area altogether when the lawn is being mowed.

☐ Don't leave a hose lying in the sun. Water in it can get hot enough to scald a child.

☐ Keep children away from the grill at all times, especially when you are cooking on it.

☐ Children should always use sunscreen and protective clothing such as hats when outside.

Backyard Grills

There is nothing more entertaining than preparing picnics in the backyard over the summer. Precautions need to be taken, however, when cooking on gas grills.

☐ Thoroughly clean gas grills at the beginning of the season. Place and at all times maintain a fire extinguisher near but not on the grill.

☐ Never throw a match in a grill, especially after the gas has been on three seconds.

☐ Never wear a loose apron or loose clothing while grilling. Always wear shoes.

☐ Always use the grill's starter button. If the starter is broken, do not use the grill.

☐ Avoid cooking foods with a high fat content, which can produce high flames. Always thoroughly cook food to a safe temperature.

☐ Never throw away grill instructions or the owner's manual. Follow manufacturer's directions carefully.

Just these few precautions can lead to safe and relaxing leisure time during warm weather.

Swimming Pools

A swimming pool can provide countless hours of fun and enjoyment. It is also one of the most dangerous single areas inside or outside your house. Many safety measures should be taken if you have a swimming pool, especially if you have children; however, even if you do not have young children or children at all, you should still take a variety of precautions, because children are very attracted to water.

Swimming pools are great fun and a good way to spend time with family and friends. Following these safety tips can help ensure that your swimming pool is as fun and safe as possible.

Swimming Pool Access—Fencing

☐ Put a fence or barrier around all four sides of your pool, so it cannot be entered directly either from the house or the play yard. The fence should be at least four feet high, with spokes and slats not more than three inches apart. If you use chain-link fencing, be sure the links are small enough so a child cannot climb on them.

☐ If the house is part of the barrier, all the doors leading from the house to the pool should be protected with an alarm and should always be locked.

☐ Encourage neighbors to keep their pools fenced and locked.

☐ If the pool is above ground, remove the ladder to prevent access by children.

☐ Never assume a pool to be safe, even if the pool has a cover or a fence surrounding it.

Swimming Pool Access—Gates and Doors

☐ Install a child-resistant spring-lock, self-closing, or self-

latching gate, with the latch about fifty-four inches from the ground, to keep children from entering the pool area.
- ☐ Install small hook-and-eye locks at the top of any exterior doors to prevent your child from unlocking the door.
- ☐ Lock windows and doors that lead to the pool from the home.
- ☐ Regularly oil the hinges and latches to ensure proper closure.
- ☐ Lock screen doors and doggie doors.

Swimming Pool Safety—Area Surrounding Pool
- ☐ Install textured concrete or other slip-resistant material around the pool.
- ☐ Put outdoor furniture inside the fenced area, so that children cannot climb onto it to enter the pool area.
- ☐ If furniture must remain outside the fenced area, padlock the pool gate and put the key above the reach of a child standing on a table or chair.

Swimming Pool Safety—Children
- ☐ Never leave a child alone in a pool. Drowning can occur in a matter of seconds.
- ☐ Be sure nothing blocks the view of the pool from the house.
- ☐ Use a water-activated pool alarm.
- ☐ Install a phone by the pool to keep from reentering the house to answer a call.
- ☐ Don't drink alcohol while you are watching children.
- ☐ Don't take a baby into a pool before it has good head control.
- ☐ Don't allow children under five in a spa or hot tub.
- ☐ Don't rely on swimming lessons to protect your child. Good swimmers can forget what to do if they are in a panic.

☐ Never allow wheeled toys in the pool area. These can be easily ridden into the water.

☐ Teach kids how to swim. Children should take a basic-level course at the age of four or five that teaches them how to get out of the water if they fall in.

☐ Do not allow roughhousing or running by the pool.

☐ Do not use glassware of any kind by the pool.

☐ Be sure that children wear life preservers if they are going to be in or near the water.

Swimming Pool Safety—General Tips

☐ Always use sunscreen.

☐ Use only battery-operated radios and televisions by the pool.

☐ Don't swim during thunderstorms.

☐ Empty wading pools when not in use. A child can drown in as little as two inches of water.

☐ Learn and practice lifesaving techniques and CPR.

Bicycle Safety

Bicycling attracts millions of riders in the United States. A great number of these bicyclists are children ages fourteen and under. When used properly, bicycles can provide a fun and enjoyable way to stay in shape, but when used without concern or in a reckless manner, injuries and fatalities can result. Bicycles are associated with more childhood injuries than any other consumer product except the automobile.

Bicycle Helmets

Recent studies have shown that using a bicycle helmet can reduce head injuries by up to 95 percent. While everyone is at risk of injury, children ages six to twelve are at the greatest risk for bicycle accidents, with injuries to the head as the most serious result. It is paramount that parents insist that their children wear bicycle helmets at all times when riding bicycles. Parents should also wear a helmet when riding, not only to act as a role model for their children, but for their own protection as well. With three out of every four bicycle-related deaths attributed to head injuries, wearing a helmet is not just an option but a necessity.

With bicycle helmets coming in all shapes and sizes, children as well as adults can find the one that fits their needs. A helmet should fit snugly, but comfortably. Parents should not purchase a helmet for their child with the intent that they eventually will grow into it. Helmets for children can be purchased with additional padding of varying thickness, which can be removed as the child's head grows. The helmet must have a chin strap and buckles that will stay securely fastened. The helmet should always fit snugly atop the head. The child should be taken to the store to be fitted properly, just as you would do for his or her shoes.

There are three nationally recognized safety standards for bicycle helmets sold in the United States, all of which are endorsed by the National Highway Traffic Safety Administration. The American National Standards Institute (ANSI), the American Society for Testing Materials (ASTM), and the Snell Memorial Foundation have each set standards and requirements for the bicycle helmet previously discussed. Helmets meeting the Snell Memorial Foundation, ASTM, or the ANSI requirements will have a label from that organization on the inside of the helmet. These helmets have been tested and will likely provide better protection from serious harm than others. If ever you are involved in a crash and the helmet is damaged, replace it or have it examined by the manufacturer or proper salesperson before reuse.

Biker Clothing

In addition to a helmet, riders must wear the proper clothing. Clothing should be of light color, and, for riding at night, clothing should be marked with reflective material. The Consumer Product Safety Commission (CPSC) suggests that individuals wear neon, fluorescent, or other bright colors when riding a bicycle. Vests, jackets, tape, wristbands, and other items that make the rider visible to motorists are widely available and can be found at most sporting goods and bike shops. Many stores carry specialty clothing that is designed especially for the most serious bicycling enthusiast.

Clothing should be close fitting to avoid getting caught in the moving parts of the bicycle. Items such as headphones, which detract from the ability to concentrate and hear traffic, should never be worn when operating a bicycle.

About Your Bike

Just like people, no two bicycles are the same. So when it comes to selecting a suitable bicycle, make sure to choose one that fits correctly. The first rule is never to ride a bike that is too big. When the bicycle is too large, your control is severely limited. Once you select the correct bicycle size, have it properly fitted. This entails adjusting the seat height and stem length. When properly fitted, the handlebar will be slightly lower than the seat. Also, make sure you can stand over the tube of your bicycle. Consult your owner's manual for proper fitting techniques and adjustments.

Bicycle baskets are a handy way to carry your necessary gear when you travel. Yet not all baskets help the bicycle perform in the same manner. Front baskets have a center of gravity that is too high. This makes for awkward steering and handling. Rear baskets tend to work better. If your bicycle is not yet equipped with a basket, use a backpack. Never carry anything in your hands that could possibly detract from your control of the bicycle. Also, watch out for objects in the basket that might dangle, like a purse strap or chain. These tend to catch in your wheels, causing damage to both the object and the bicycle.

Child seats for bikes are another concern. Parents are encouraged to have their children ride with them, but always to ensure safety at every step. Make sure a child's feet will not be caught in the wheels. Baby seats with only stirrups are dangerous. Children's feet can easily become entangled in the spokes, causing serious harm. Look for those that provide actual inserts for children's feet as opposed to stirrups. Also, make sure that the child's seat is securely attached. Child seats have been known to fall off a moving bicycle.

Before ever using your bicycle, check to make sure all parts are secure and working well. The handlebars should be firmly in place and should turn easily. Also, the wheels should be straight and secure. If your bicycle has quick-release wheels, it is your responsibility as a cyclist to make sure that they are firmly closed at all times and to use the safety retainer if there is one. Always check the wheels before riding, after any fall, or after transporting your bicycle. If at any time you are unsure or have any questions concerning your bicycle, consult the owner's manual or speak with your bicycle dealer.

Obeying Traffic Laws and Rules

Did you know that a bicycle, when ridden on the streets, is considered a vehicle, and not a toy? In most jurisdictions, "every person riding a bicycle upon a roadway has all the rights and duties applicable to the driver of a vehicle." Just like a vehicle driver, a cyclist must follow and adhere to all traffic laws that apply to motor vehicle operators. As a motorist, a bicycle rider must not only be aware of his or her own driving, but the driving of others as well. The key to all successful driving is staying alert. Watch for potholes, cracks, railroad tracks, wet leaves, and drainage grates. Also, be on the lookout for low traffic signs, loose gravel and broken glass, oil slicks, and unmarked posts as possible obstacles that could cause you to fall.

Before going around an object, scan ahead and behind you for a break or gap in the traffic. Plan your move strategically and then signal your move. Once your move has been signaled, quickly but cautiously execute your plan. If you are unsure of the area or are not comfortable with your present skill level in a rough patch, pull off to the right side of the road and walk your bicycle around the troublesome area.

Be especially careful in wet weather and in areas where there could be ice or frost in your path. These are places that are slipping and injury likely could occur. Apply the same caution when crossing bridges and railroad tracks. When approaching a railroad track, use extreme caution, crossing at a ninety-degree angle.

Many people have been taught to go against the normal flow of traffic. In reality, nothing could be more dangerous. Always ride on the right side with the traffic, in a straight and predictable path. Proceed in a single-file line if traveling with more than one bicyclist. When you ride against the flow of traffic, you put yourself in a position where other motorists are not expecting you to be.

Young children, typically under the age of nine, are not yet able to identify and adjust to many hazardous traffic situations. Therefore, they should not be allowed to ride in the street unsupervised. Children who are permitted to ride in the street without supervision should have the necessary skills to safely follow the traffic laws and rules of the road.

Did you know that over 70 percent of all car-bicycle accidents occur in driveways or at intersections? Before you enter any street, always check for traffic. Look left, then right, then left again, walking your bicycle into the street to begin the ride. If you are already in the street, always look behind you for a break in the traffic, then signal before going left or right. Also be aware of left- or right-turning traffic. When going through an intersection, never follow a large truck or car closely. This keeps you out of view, hidden from others and in threat of terrible danger. Wait your turn at intersections. Whether you are going straight or turning right, do not pass a car on the right. Even if you are in a bicycle lane, a car beside you might not notice and might make a right turn without signaling.

Just as any automobile operator must do, be courteous to all pedestrians and other vehicle operators. Become familiar with the accommodations that are available for bicyclists in your area. These include bicycle lanes and routes as well as off-road paths. Be smart and take advantage of these whenever possible. Remember, being courteous involves using the bike lane and streets if possible and leaving the sidewalks for pedestrians. Pedestrians always have the right of way. And if you need to pass a pedestrian, always do so to the right, calling out your plan of action loudly and before you get to the person that you are passing.

Another area of concern is speed. Always control your speed by using your brakes. Never reach a speed that you are not able to control. When the hand brake is fully applied, it should not touch the handlebars. Each brake-shoe pad should wear down evenly and never be separated more than one eighth of an inch from the rim.

Riding at Night

As with any recreational sport or exercise, bicycling at night is extremely dangerous. Most bicycles are equipped for daylight use and need to be adapted for use in the nighttime. If you must ride at night, the following precautionary measures should be taken:

- ☐ Ride with reflectors. Make sure the reflectors meet CPSC requirements. These laws state that reflectors be on the front and rear of the bicycle, on the pedals, and on the wheels. Wheel reflectors can be reflective tire sidewalls, reflective wheel rims, or spoke mounted. These reflectors should be permanently installed on bicycles for daytime use also.

- ☐ Add the brightest lights possible to both the front and the back of the bicycle. These lights not only help you to see better, but they also increase the visibility of the bicycle for other road users and may be required by law in certain jurisdictions.

- ☐ As noted earlier, wear reflective clothing or material—especially on your ankles, wrists, back, and helmet.

☐ Ride only in areas familiar to you. Brightly lit streets are the best. Always assume that the drivers of other vehicles cannot see you.

Education and Training Programs

Parents are encouraged to enroll their children in bicycle training classes. Parents, along with schools, should work out safety programs that should include safe routes to and from school. Local police departments are always interested in providing bicycle education programs to children. State highway safety offices are good sources of additional information.

Conclusion

Bicycling is a great way to stay fit and enjoy the outdoors. With a few precautionary measures, biking can be a lifetime activity, enjoyed by the whole family. Please, take the time to prepare yourself and others by learning a few simple guidelines about being safe on the streets and the bike trails.

Sports and Recreational Safety

Each year it seems our country is becoming more and more conscious about living a healthy lifestyle. From young to young at heart, people of all ages are getting out and getting fit. With so many forms of recreational sports and activities, people have more options to choose from than in years past. Making exercise fun and enjoyable is a necessity, but an aspect just as important as enjoyment is safety from hazards that could cause serious injury. For a safe recreational experience, please follow the guidelines listed below for the selected sports and recreational activities to ensure that you participate in your chosen activity as safely as possible.

Team Sport Safety Tips

For any sport in which you participate, there are safety tips you should follow to ensure hazard-free fun.

Baseball
- ☐ Learn the fundamentals of the sport.
- ☐ Always wear a snug-fitting helmet when at bat.
- ☐ Before swinging a bat, be sure you are in a safe place, with no one near you.
- ☐ Be sure that the person you are throwing the ball to is ready to catch it.
- ☐ Learn how to properly dodge the ball. Step away from the plate and turn your back to wild pitches, throws, or uncatchable hits.

Football
- ☐ When tackling, never lead with your helmet.
- ☐ Be sure to wear proper equipment and check to ensure it is not damaged.
- ☐ Play with other people of approximately your same size and ability level.

In-Line Skating
- ☐ Always wear wrist guards, knee pads, and elbow pads to help prevent injury.
- ☐ Always wear a helmet.
- ☐ Don't skate in the street.
- ☐ Skate with other people.
- ☐ Make sure the brakes are in good working order.

Soccer
- ☐ Goals should be firmly fastened to the ground.
- ☐ Wear shin guards.

☐ Shoelaces should be tied securely and the bow should be tucked into shoe tops.

☐ Remove nets when goals are not in use and disassemble goals for seasonal storage.

Skateboarding

Skateboarding is one of the most popular sports for teenagers today. It involves good balance and body control. Yet, many skateboarders are young enough not to have fully developed the necessary skills and quick reflexes to skate safely. Sadly, skateboarding can be quite dangerous. Follow these tips for safe skateboarding:

☐ Always check the skateboard for hazards, such as loose, broken, or cracked parts; sharp edges on metal boards; slippery top surfaces; and wheels with nicks and cracks.

☐ Always watch out for holes, rocks, bumps, and debris.

☐ Always wear protective gear, such as helmets and pads.

☐ Never ride on the street.

☐ Never hitch a ride from a car or other motor vehicle.

☐ Relax rather than stiffen the body in the event of a fall.

☐ If you are losing your balance, crouch down.

☐ If you are falling, try to land on the fleshy parts of your body.

☐ Try to roll rather than catch yourself with your arms when falling.

Boats and Jet Skis

Warm weather can be a lot of fun, but families should take a few precautionary steps to limit seasonal risks. The Independent Insurance Agents of America (IIAA) offers the following tips to help make your summer a happy and safe one:

Boats

☐ Never use a boat that is not equipped with fully operational safety equipment. At a minimum, any boat should contain life preservers for all occupants, a well-stocked first aid kit, powerful flashlight, two-way VHF radio, fire extinguisher, flare kit, and local-area water chart. Large boats should also contain additional lines of varied size and an inflatable lifeboat.

☐ Never exceed the passenger capacity recommended by the manufacturer and always keep all owner's manuals onboard.

☐ Take a boat safety and operations course sponsored in many communities by the U.S. Power Squadron or Coast Guard.

Jet Skis

☐ No one under age eight should ever ride a Jet Ski.

☐ Never use a Jet Ski in foul weather.

☐ Strictly follow all safety guidelines and make sure anyone driving the vehicle knows exactly how to operate it and shut it off.

Common Minor Sports Injuries

Most sports injuries are preventable. To assist in avoiding injuries, participants should exercise regularly, train adequately, use the correct equipment and clothing, and cease activity as soon as a suspected injury occurs. Sports can require contact, or they can be noncontact activities. In either case, injuries can occur, and there can be many different kinds. Most of the following injuries require first aid; however, for other ones, a visit to the doctor's office is recommended.

- Chest cramps (or "stitches"). Brought on by exertion, chest cramps are identified by sharp chest pains, difficulty in standing upright, and gasping for breath. Rest and deep breathing will usually result in the cramps going away.
- Corked thigh. Caused by a blow to the thigh, this condition

occurs when the injured muscle contracts and becomes "tight." It is very painful and may include a loss of the ability to move the limb. Rest, an ice pack, a bandage, slight exercise, and stretching help to manage the pain.

- Groin and testicle injuries. Caused by a blow or strain to the groin. It is characterized by pain around the groin, sometimes nausea or vomiting, and the inability to stand upright. The victim should be placed on his back with knees slightly bent and have an ice pack applied with caution to the injury site, and medical aid should be sought.

- Muscle cramps. Muscle cramps are caused by overstretching muscles or by sweating. Cramps can be identified as pain, tenderness, a loss of power, and stiffening of the muscles. They should be treated with rest, an ice pack, and slight stretching. Don't massage.

- Shin splints. This injury is caused by the strain of the muscle of the toes and is characterized by pain up and down the shin. People who play football or run track are common victims. It should be treated with rest, an ice pack, and elevation of the limb.

- Tennis elbow. The straining of the tendons and muscles around the elbow causes this injury. If it occurs often, the elbow is overused and overstretched. The victim will have a pain centered over the bone on the outer side of the joint that becomes more severe on movement. To treat, use an ice pack and a sling and get medical help.

- Winding. Caused by a strong blow to the abdomen and characterized by breathing difficulty, gasping attempts to breathe, and lack of chest movement or bending. The victim should assume a reclining position and rest.

PART 3

THE COMMUNITY

12

SCHOOL SAFETY: IMPROVING YOUR CHILD'S SAFETY AT SCHOOL

A truck hauling thirty-eight tons of steel crashed into the side of a Michigan school bus, injuring forty-eight children and adults. The truck rammed into the side of the bus, spinning it around three times before pushing it about one hundred feet and tearing a hole in its side.

Preventing School Violence

 Since the tragedy at Columbine High School, school violence has been a hot topic across the country. Every parent wants to send their child to a school where he or she can learn in a safe environment. Precautions can be taken to prevent the possibility of school violence happening at your child's school.

Schools play a pivotal role in helping students develop good social skills, and individual relationships are critical to that socialization process. Personalization can create contexts to counter violence.

Smaller classes allow education professionals to form steady, caring relationships with the students most likely to perpetrate or suffer from physical and psychological violence.

School violence frequently results from conflicts that are inappropriately managed and then intensify. Conflict resolution programs, properly designed and implemented, offer students and educators the skills to constructively handle controversies that naturally arise in learning situations. Beyond helping students learn how to manage conflicts, schools must also foster the cultivation of good character. Approaches to reducing school violence are most effective when they are congruent with teaching and overall learning. Just as schools reflect the broader communities they serve, they must also work with those communities to prevent violence.

There are things parents can do to ensure the safety of their child's school. Parents should ask these questions at their child's school:

- ☐ Is my school responsive to all children?
- ☐ Has my school taken steps to ensure that all staff, students, and families understand the principles underlying the identification of early-warning signs?
- ☐ Has my school taken steps to ensure that all staff, students, and families know how to identify and respond to imminent warning signs?
- ☐ Does my school understand the principles underlying intervention?
- ☐ Does my school make early intervention available for students at risk of behavioral problems?
- ☐ Does my school have preventive strategies in place that support early intervention?
- ☐ Does my school have a procedure for intervening during a crisis to ensure safety?

☐ Does my school know how to respond in the aftermath of tragedy?

(Sources: *Preventing School Violence: Policies for Safety, Caring and Achievement,* <http://www.ascd.org/readingroom/infobrief/96autumn .htm>; School Violence Prevention Check List, <http://familyeducation .com/article/0%2C1120%2C1-6471%2C00.html>)

School Fire Safety

Children should know what to do in case of a fire and how they can help prevent fires from starting. There are fire hazards hidden all over your child's school. Here are just a few examples:

☐ Papier-mâché sculptures in hallways.

☐ Many posters and much paper artwork on the walls.

☐ Halloween haunted houses in school gyms jammed with scary decorations.

☐ Stockpiles of old chemicals in high school science labs.

☐ Heavily amplified concerts with miles of electric cables.

☐ Old space heaters and electric coffee pots in faculty lounges.

☐ Overstuffed furniture designed to make kids feel at home in classrooms and offices.

Parents can help monitor schools to assess fire hazards in their child's school. Additionally, children should know what to do when there is a fire at their school.

☐ Know the escape plan and be orderly. The teacher should tell students how to line up to leave the room when the alarm sounds.

- ☐ Know where you are going and learn which exit to use. The teacher should show students a "meeting place" outside the school building where they are to go after they've escaped.
- ☐ Plan to help others, including students who need special help, to leave the building.
- ☐ Know two ways to get out of the school. Every room should have a map posted showing at least two ways out to enable an escape even if one exit is blocked.
- ☐ Know the alarm sound. The school fire alarm—a bell, a buzzer, or a horn—should sound different from an ambulance, fire truck, police-car siren, or the usual school bell. Students should learn its sound so they can quickly respond.
- ☐ Everyone should stop what they're doing and listen. When the fire alarm sounds, listen to teachers or adult supervisors in case there are more instructions about which exit to use.
- ☐ Exit safely. Walk out of the classroom quickly and quietly in an orderly line. Do not run. Walk to the exit and go to the designated meeting place outside the building. Stay with the group and do not leave the meeting place until the teacher has seen you.
- ☐ Don't go back inside for anything. Wait until authorities say it's safe to go back inside.
- ☐ Know what to do if you cannot follow your original exit plan.

(Sources: *Bucks County Courier Times,* <http://www.phillyburbs.com /couriertimes/webspecials/fire/paperchases.html>; School Fire Drills, <http://www.firestation24.com/drill/htm>)

School Bus Safety

School buses have become one of the safest forms of transportation, but they could be even safer. Buses are designed to withstand all but the most serious crashes without death or serious injury, according to the National School Transportation Association. School buses should be made safer by having seat belts installed.

The majority of accidents take place outside the school bus in the "danger zone" that surrounds every school bus. This zone is located in two main areas—the rear and side of the school bus where children exit the bus and the front of the school bus where children cross the street. If children bend down to pick up something they've dropped in these areas, the bus driver cannot see them. To combat this, many children are taught to take five giant steps when they get off the school bus to get out of the danger zone.

Here are additional safety tips to keep your child safe around the school bus:

- [ ] When waiting for the bus, children should stay away from traffic, should avoid roughhousing or other careless behavior, and should not stray onto streets, alleys, or private property.
- [ ] Children should line up away from the road as the school bus approaches. They should wait until the bus has stopped and the door has opened before stepping on.
- [ ] Children should use the handrail when stepping onto the bus.
- [ ] When on the bus, children should find a seat and sit down. Loud talking or other noise that can distract the bus driver should not be allowed. They should never put their heads, arms, or hands out of the window.
- [ ] Children should keep aisles clear of books or bags.

- ☐ Before reaching their stop, children should get ready to exit by getting books and belongings together.
- ☐ At their stop, they should wait for the bus to stop completely before getting up from their seats. Only then should they walk to the front door and exit, using the handrail.
- ☐ If children have to cross the street in front of the bus, they should walk at least ten feet ahead of the bus along the side of the road until they can turn around and see the driver and wait for his or her signal before beginning to cross.
- ☐ They should not cross the centerline of the road until the driver has signaled that it is safe for them to begin walking.
- ☐ They should stay away from the bus's rear wheels at all times.

The bus can be a dangerous place for a child, but if they follow these tips and are aware of their surroundings, children can have a safe trip. Remind children always to be alert and to follow the directions of their bus driver to avoid an accident or injury.

(Source: NHTSA's Safety City Bus Safety, <http://www.nhtsa.dot.gov/kids/bussafety/>)

Backpacks

Did you know that your child's favorite backpack could lead to permanent back pain? In an October 1999 survey of more than one hundred orthopedic surgeons conducted by the American Academy of Orthopedic Surgeons, 58 percent of the orthopedists reported seeing patients complaining of back and shoulder pain caused by heavy backpacks.

By the end of their teen years, more than half of youths experience at least one lower-back-pain episode. The Consumer Product Safety Commission estimates that 4,928 emergency room visits each year result from injuries related to book bags and back carriers.

Here are some tips to keep your child's back in good shape:

- [ ] The weight of a child's backpack should not exceed 15 percent of the child's body weight. For example, if a child weighs eighty pounds, he or she should carry no more than twelve pounds in his or her backpack.
- [ ] Consider more than looks when choosing a backpack. A backpack that does not fit correctly can cause back pain, muscle strain, or nerve impingement.
- [ ] Use a backpack with wide padded straps and a padded back. Use a hip strap for heavier weights.
- [ ] Use both of the backpack's straps, firmly tightened to hold the pack two inches above the waist.
- [ ] Have your children condition their back muscles. Ask an orthopedic surgeon for advice.
- [ ] Use correct lifting techniques.
  - — Face the backpack before you lift it.
  - — Bend at the knees.
  - — Using both hands, check the weight of the pack.
  - — Lift with your legs, not your back.
  - — Carefully put one shoulder strap on at a time. Never sling the pack onto one shoulder.
- [ ] Place the heaviest items close to your back.
- [ ] Neatly pack your backpack and try to keep items in place.
- [ ] Try to make frequent trips to your locker between classes to replace books.
- [ ] Consider purchasing a backpack with wheels.
- [ ] Purchase a second set of books for home.

By following these steps you can help your child stay healthy. Back pain can follow a person throughout a lifetime, so it is important to keep an eye on your child's backpack—how much it weighs and how it's carried.

(Sources: Backpack Safety America, <http://www.backpacksafe.com /safety.htm>; American Academy of Orthopedic Surgeons, <http://www. aaos.org>)

Latchkey Children

About one third of all school-age children, an estimated five million between ages five and thirteen in the United States, are so-called latchkey children—kids who care for themselves after school while parents are at work. Many parents struggle with determining if their child is ready or old enough to be left alone at home. Here are some questions that can help you determine the readiness of your child.

- ☐ Does the child want to be on his or her own?
- ☐ Is he or she afraid to be alone in the house?
- ☐ Can you depend on him or her to follow the house rules?
- ☐ Does he or she complete his or her assigned chores as agreed?
- ☐ Can you rely on him or her to tell the truth?
- ☐ Does he or she have common sense?
- ☐ Can he or she deal with unexpected situations in a positive way?
- ☐ Is he or she self-motivated?
- ☐ Can he or she amuse him- or herself or does he or she require constant supervision?

Once you have determined that your child is ready to stay at home alone here are some guidelines to keep your child safe at home:

- ☐ The telephone is the lifeline between working parents and their children. To reduce anxiety, have your child phone you as soon as he or she arrives home. Parents should call children periodically to check on them.

☐ It is helpful for parents to keep the amount of time their children spend alone each day to a minimum. Three hours a day pushes the limit of what most children can handle.

☐ Accidents are the main cause of death in children under twelve. Teach your children basic first aid procedures and instruct them how to call for an ambulance or the fire department. Practice a fire drill and make sure your home has working smoke detectors and a working fire extinguisher.

☐ Helpful neighbors can be the key to a successful latchkey experience. They can assist children in emergencies and provide moral support. Parents should select trustworthy neighbors who are willing to help, if needed, and who are reasonably close by and usually home during after-school hours.

☐ Boredom is often a problem among latchkey kids. Children need scheduled activities.

☐ Make sure your doors have secure deadbolts and are locked until parents come home.

☐ Make sure important phone numbers are posted next to the telephone.

By following these tips, your child can have a safe after-school experience!

(Sources: Home Alone: Tips for Latchkey Kids, <http://www.click10.com/mia/health/summerofsafety/stories/summerofsafety-149531320020604-110655.html>; At Home, Alone: Safety Tips for Latchkey Children, <http://www.cfc.efc.ca/docs/mcca/00001_en.htm>;Latch Key Issues: Tips for a Safe & Healthy Back to School Routine, <http://www.fultondailynews.com/news/2000/081400/081900/lmh_latchkeys.html>)

13

College Safety: Tips for the College Student

A university student said she felt compelled to be thin and to control her eating when she first arrived at college. She later developed an eating disorder.

Although bacterial meningitis is rare, studies suggest students who live in college dormitories, especially college freshmen, are up to six times more likely to get meningitis than students living off campus.

Dorm Fire Safety

 Students can take steps to ensure their safety while living in dormitories. Here are some important tips:

☐   Be sure you have individual smoke and carbon monoxide detectors in your room.

- ☐ If you hear a smoke detector or fire alarm go off, do not ignore it. Exit the dorm immediately and call 911.
- ☐ Do not overload electrical outlets.
- ☐ Do not disable smoke alarms, even while cooking. Students smoking or cooking in rooms often disable alarms; thus nearly 10 percent fail to signal dorm fires. Cooking in dorm rooms accounts for about 18 percent of dorm fires.
- ☐ Install safety grilles on halogen torchères. These lights produce a lot of heat and can easily ignite nearby fabric.
- ☐ Be careful with candles and incense. Candles and burning incense cause about twelve thousand residential fires annually. Never leave a lighted candle unattended.
- ☐ Do not smoke in a dorm room. Smoking is the third greatest cause of dorm fires.
- ☐ Note the fire emergency routes closest to your room and take a practice run.

(Sources: Security World, <http://www.securityworld.com/library/ college/dormfiresafety.html>; College Fire Safety, <http://www.collegefire safety.org>)

Student Travel

Travel is a favorite hobby in the United States, and many students choose to study abroad to expand their college experience. Steps can be taken to avoid blunders and make your travels more fun.

Staying out of legal trouble is a must. "Each year 2,500 American citizens are arrested abroad—about half on narcotics charges, including possession of very small amounts of illegal substances," says the U.S. Department of State Bureau of Consular Affairs. A drug may be legal in one country, but illegal in another. "Some young people are victimized because they may be unaware of the laws, customs, or standards of the country they are visiting."

Additionally, young Americans have suffered injuries and even death as a result of automobile accidents, drowning, falls, and other accidents. Motor vehicle crashes are a leading cause of injury among travelers, so walk and drive carefully, advises Karen Minich of <http://www.smarterliving.com>.

It is recommended that travelers make copies of passports, credit cards, and other documents and leave them with a family member or friend in case of an emergency.

Sightseeing

When sightseeing and walking around a city, it is important to be aware of your surroundings. Here are some tips to keep you safe in the city:

- [ ] Walk like you know where you're going, even if you don't.
- [ ] If you get lost, ask for directions from a shop clerk, not a random person on the street.
- [ ] Plan out your trip the night before, and if possible, get directions at your hotel or hostel.
- [ ] Don't roam the streets with a map in one hand, a guide-book under your arm, and a camera around your neck. Carry items in a bag. Use your guidebook while you're seated in a restaurant. Carry a whistle.
- [ ] Don't hand your camera to just anyone when you're ready to take a photo. Find another tourist—preferably one with a family. He or she probably won't run off with your camera. Also consider buying a disposable camera.
- [ ] Avoid dark alleys and dead-end streets.
- [ ] If you want to drink heavily, do so in your hotel or nearby. You can lose your sense of direction and get lost if you are not close to where you are staying. It is also wise to drink with friends and not strangers.
- [ ] Check out travel advisories from the U.S. State Depart-

ment at <http://www.travel.state.gov/travel_warnings
.html>.

Money and Exchange Rates

- ☐ Use credit cards or ATM cards for your purchases, when possible. The exchange rate is usually better on a credit card than for traveler's checks. For up-to-date currency exchange rates, go to <http://www.xe.net/ucc/>.
- ☐ It is a good idea to convert about $50 to $100 into local currency at your first destination. It will save you time if you already have some money converted.

Health and Food

- ☐ Get immunization shots if they are needed for your destination.
- ☐ Drink bottled water. Use bottled water to brush your teeth and for hygiene.
- ☐ Eat only thoroughly cooked food. Don't eat raw fruits and vegetables.
- ☐ Don't forget to carry antacid or stomach medicine. Foreign foods or foods you've never eaten before can upset your stomach.
- ☐ Prescriptions are drugs and are treated as such overseas. Make sure prescriptions stay in their proper bottles and that you have copies of your prescriptions with you.
- ☐ Sunblock isn't an extra. It's a must.
- ☐ Take comfortable shoes if you plan on walking a lot.

Preventing Disease

- ☐ Wash hands often with soap and water or use antiseptic hand cleanser.

☐ Don't eat or drink dairy products unless you know they have been pasteurized.

☐ Never eat undercooked ground beef, poultry, or eggs.

Following these tips, you can make your trip safer and more enjoyable.

(Sources: Karen Minich at Smarter Living, <http://www.smarterliving .com>; U.S. Department of State Bureau of Consular Affairs, <http://travel .state.gov>)

Meningitis

Bacterial meningitis is becoming increasingly prevalent on college campuses across the United States. It is an infection of the fluid around the spinal cord and brain that causes flulike symptoms. If it is not detected early, the disease can progress, often within hours of the first signs of symptoms.

The disease itself is rare, but studies suggest that students who live in dormitories at college, especially freshmen, are up to six times more likely to get meningitis than students who live off campus. It is estimated that 100 to 125 cases of meningococcal meningitis occur annually on college campuses and that five to fifteen students die as a result.

This type of meningitis is transmitted through air droplets and direct contact with infected persons. Studies have shown that fifteen- to twenty-four-year-olds are at greatest risk of getting meningococcal meningitis. Many students live in crowded conditions in dorms and are under stress from school.

The Centers for Disease Control and the American College Health Association recommend vaccinations, especially for freshmen living in dormitories and for any other students who wish to reduce their risk of contracting meningitis. Protection lasts approximately three to five years—the length of time most students are away at college. The vaccine costs about $60 and is 80 to 90 percent effective.

Meningococcal disease, caused by the bacterium *Neisseria meningitidis,* can result in hearing loss, kidney failure, amputation of the limbs, and permanent brain injury. In the event of meningococcal disease, antibiotics can be effective, but treatment must begin immediately. Outbreaks of the disease usually occur in late winter or early spring—when college classes are in session. The best way to protect students is to have them vaccinated.

(Sources: Meningitis Foundation of America, <http://ww.musa.org>; Centers for Disease Control, <http://www.cdc.gov>; Kids Source, <http://www.kidsource.com/health/meningococcal.html>; CNN.com, <http://www.cnn.com/US/9910/20/college.meningitis>; <http://www.cnn.com/HEALTH/9905/25/college.meningitis/index.html>)

Eating Disorders

Over the past several years, the number of college students developing eating disorders has risen. A 1992 Harvard study revealed that one in five undergraduates has an eating disorder. Eating disorders tend to be coping mechanisms. Many college students are under a lot of stress during the transition to college life, schoolwork, jobs, and new responsibilities. Some students find that eating is one thing they can control.

In developed societies, anorexia nervosa and bulimia are the two most common eating disorders.

Anorexia Nervosa

People with anorexia are described as having low self-esteem and feeling that others are controlling their lives, according to the Food and Drug Administration. Some anorexics may be very overactive, for example, exercising excessively despite fatigue. Their preoccupation with food usually prompts strange food-related patterns or rituals such as crumbling food, moving it about on the plate, cutting it into very tiny pieces to prolong meals, and not eating with the rest of the family. People with anorexia sometimes become gourmet cooks, preparing elaborate meals for others, while eating low-calorie food themselves.

Anorexic individuals become obsessed with a fear of fat and with losing weight. In their mind's eye, they see normal folds of flesh as fat that must be eliminated. They may have trouble sleeping. Because there's no longer a fat tissue padding, sitting or lying down brings discomfort rather than rest. As their obsession increasingly controls their lives, they may withdraw from friends.

All the following criteria must be met for a case to be recognized as anorexia nervosa:

☐ Intense fear of becoming obese even when underweight.

☐ Disturbance in the way in which one's body weight, size, or shape is experienced, for example, claiming to "feel fat" even when emaciated, believing that one area of the body is "too fat" even when obviously underweight.

☐ Refusal to maintain body weight over a minimal normal weight for age and height, for example, weight loss leading to a body weight 15 percent below expected and failure to gain expected weight during period of growth.

☐ In females, absence of at least three consecutive menstrual cycles when otherwise expected to occur. Primary amenorrhea is diagnosed when menstruation fails to occur at puberty, while secondary amenorrhea occurs when menstruation ceases after normal onset.

Many of the anorexic's peculiar behaviors and bodily changes are typical of any starvation victim, but most functions are often restored to normal when sufficient weight is regained. Meanwhile, the starving body tries to protect itself, especially the brain and the heart, by slowing down or stopping less-vital body processes. Menstruation ceases, often before weight loss becomes noticeable; blood pressure and respiratory rate slow down; and thyroid function diminishes, resulting in brittle hair and nails, dry skin, slowed pulse rate, cold intolerance, and constipation. With the depletion of fat, the body temperature is lowered. Soft hair, called lanugo, forms over the skin. Electrolyte imbalance can become so severe that irregular heart rhythm, heart failure, and decreased bone density occur. Other physical signs and symptoms can include mild anemia, swelling of joints, reduced muscle mass, and lightheadedness.

Bulimia

Bulimia ordinarily begins between the ages of seventeen and twenty-five. However, because many bulimics are deeply ashamed of their bingeing and purging and keep these activities a guarded secret, an actual diagnosis may not be made until patients are well into their thirties or forties. Bulimia usually begins in conjunction with a diet. But once the binge-purge cycle becomes established, it can get out of control. Some bulimics may be somewhat underweight and a few may be obese, but most tend to keep a nearly normal weight. In many, the menstrual cycle becomes irregular. Sexual interest may diminish. Bulimics may exhibit impulsive behaviors such as shoplifting and alcohol and drug abuse. Many appear to be healthy and successful, perfectionists at whatever they do. Actually, most bulimics have very low self-esteem and are often depressed.

Binges may last eight hours and result in an intake of 20,000 calories. One study, however, showed the average binge to be slightly less than one and a quarter hours and slightly more than 3,400 calories. Most binges are carried out in secret. Bulimics often spend $50 or more a day on food and may even steal food or money to support the obsession.

To lose the gained weight, the bulimic begins purging, which may include laxatives, from fifty to one hundred or more tablets at one time, or diuretics to increase urination. Self-induced vomiting occurs by gagging, using an emetic, or simply mentally willing the action. Between binges, the person may fast or exercise excessively.

Bulimia's binge-purge cycle can be devastating to health in a number of ways. It can upset the body's balance of electrolytes such as sodium, magnesium, potassium, and calcium, resulting in fatigue, seizures, muscle cramps, irregular heartbeat, and decreased bone density, leading to osteoporosis. Repeated vomiting can damage the esophagus and stomach, cause the salivary glands to swell, make the gums recede, and erode tooth enamel. In some cases, all of the teeth must be pulled prematurely because of the constant wash by gastric acid. Other effects may be rashes, broken blood vessels in the cheeks, and swelling around the eyes, ankles, and feet.

Bulimia is diagnosed when all of the following criteria are met:

☐ Recurrent episodes of binge eating—rapid consumption of a large quantity of food in two or less hours.
☐ Feeling of lack of control over eating behavior.
☐ The individual regularly engages in self-induced vomiting, use of laxatives, or rigorous dieting or fasting in order to counteract the effects of the binge eating.
☐ A minimum average of two binge-eating episodes per week for at least three months.

Tips

So what can parents do if their child shows signs of an eating disorder? Here are some tips provided by the American Anorexia/Bulimia Association, Inc.:

☐ Do not urge your child to eat, watch him or her eat, or discuss food intake with him or her. Your involvement with your child's eating is his or her tool to manipulate you.

☐ Do not allow yourself to feel guilty. Once you have checked out your child's physical condition with a physician and made counseling available, getting well is his or her responsibility.

☐ Do not neglect your spouse or other children. Focusing on the sick child can perpetuate the illness and destroy the family.

☐ Do not be afraid to have the child separated from you, either at school or in separate housing, if it becomes obvious that the child's continued presence is undermining the emotional health of the family. Don't allow him or her to intimidate the family with threats of suicide. But don't ignore the threats either.

☐ Do not put the child down by comparing him or her to more "successful" siblings or friends. Do not ask questions such as "How are you feeling?" or "How is your social life?"

☐ Love your child as you should love yourself.

☐ Trust your child to find his or her own values, ideals, and standards, rather than insisting on yours.

☐ Do everything to encourage your child's initiative, independence, and autonomy.

☐ Be aware of the long-term nature of the illness. Families must face months and sometimes years of treatment and anxiety.

(Sources: *Eating Disorders: When Thinness Becomes an Obsession,* <http://www.nau.edu/~fronske/eatdis.html>; The Eating Disorders Site, <http://closetoyou.org/eatingdisorders>; *Something Fishy,* <http://www. something-fishy.org/default.php>)

Alcohol Abuse

Alcohol is the most widely used drug on American college and university campuses. Many of the nation's twelve million undergraduate students will die from alcohol-related causes while in school.

Because alcohol is so widely used on college campuses, it is important to be educated on the effects of alcohol.

Factors That Can Influence the Effects of Alcohol

- [ ] Drinking on an empty stomach speeds up the effects of alcohol.
- [ ] The higher the percentage of alcohol, the faster the impairment. If alcohol is mixed with food-based products such as juice or milk, it slows down the impairment. If alcohol is mixed with water or carbonated beverages, it speeds up impairment.
- [ ] Many over-the-counter medications, such as cold medications, antihistamines, and aspirin, can speed up the effects of alcohol. The same is true of illegal drugs.
- [ ] Consuming alcohol when either excited or depressed causes impairment to occur more quickly.
- [ ] One drink on the plane is equivalent to two on the ground.
- [ ] Impairment can happen faster when drinking after even a minor illness or a significant lack of sleep.
- [ ] Older people and adolescents cannot metabolize alcohol as quickly and can be impaired faster.
- [ ] Females have more fat content and therefore feel the effects of alcohol faster and stay impaired longer.
- [ ] Smaller bodies have smaller livers that may not be able to metabolize the normal half ounce of pure alcohol (the amount in an average drink) per hour. In addition, the more fat content you have, the faster you will become impaired.
- [ ] Females will become impaired more quickly for three or four days before menstruation and if they are on oral contraceptives.

Problems Caused by Drinking

Anyone who drinks to the level of impairment is at risk for a multitude of problems. These problems range from relationship issues, decrease in performance levels, reduction in abstract mental functioning, cumulative organ damage, increased occurrence of date and acquaintance rape, unplanned and unprotected sex, legal problems, automobile crashes, alcoholism, and early death.

When to Get Medical Attention

At some point, you may find yourself in a situation where someone will need medical help because of intoxication. It is important that you recognize these signs and immediately get medical care if the individual:

- ☐ Is unable to stand or walk, or can do so only with difficulty
- ☐ Is breathing slowly and shallowly
- ☐ Is passed out or in a stupor
- ☐ Has fever or chills
- ☐ Has difficulty speaking
- ☐ Has an injury
- ☐ Is paranoid, confused, or disoriented
- ☐ Is violent or threatening
- ☐ Appears to be a risk to him- or herself or others
- ☐ Appears to be dehydrated and has a bluish tint to the lips and fingernails

Avoiding Alcohol Abuse

If you or your friends are going to be drinking, it is important to be responsible. Here are some useful tips to avoid some of the health problems associated with drinking.

- [ ] Say "No, thank you" if you do not want to drink. If you would feel more comfortable with something in your hand, you can drink a nonalcoholic beverage.
- [ ] Be sure you know the alcohol content of mixed drinks and punches before you drink them.
- [ ] Count the number of drinks you consume and "pace" your drinking.
- [ ] Avoid drinking on an empty stomach. Food slows down the absorption of alcohol.
- [ ] Avoid drinking games, doing shots, and "funneling." These promote abuse of alcohol as well as abuse of one's body.
- [ ] Dilute mixed drinks, or add ice cubes and drink slowly.
- [ ] Do not drink if you are going to drive.
- [ ] Dress warmly in cold weather. Although alcohol may make you feel warm, there is an increased risk of frostbite and hypothermia from exposure to the elements after drinking, particularly if you pass out or fall asleep outside during the winter months.

(Sources: The University of Georgia Police Department, <http://www.ps.uga.edu>; The University of Georgia Health Center, <http://www.uhs.uga.edu>)

Date Rape and Sexual Assault

The typical image of the rapist is that of a crazed stranger jumping out of a dark alley and forcing a woman to have sex. The reality is that most rapes involve people who know each other and are inflicted by someone the victim trusts enough to be alone with. Acquaintance rape is when someone you know forces you to have sexual intercourse against your will, whether you are passed out, too drunk to refuse, too scared to argue, or for some other reason do not give consent.

Acquaintance rape is a form of sexual assault. Other forms of sexual assault include unwanted touching of another person's buttocks, breasts, penis, or vagina; forced penetration of genital or anal opening with an object; and unwanted sexual comments, jokes, and gestures.

Although much of the information about sexual assault and date rape focuses on an incident between a man and a woman, it also applies to assaults between men, which account for about 10 percent of all rapes.

Alcohol plays a major role in sexual assaults between college students.

Here are some surprising statistics provided by the University of Georgia Health Center:

- Almost 50 percent of unplanned sexual encounters occur while under the influence of alcohol.
- Eighty percent of first sexual experiences occur while under the influence of alcohol.
- By senior year, 81 percent of students have had sex because they were drunk.
- College students who mix alcohol and sex report having more partners whom they know only "slightly" or "moderately."
- In two-thirds of unplanned pregnancies, the woman was intoxicated during sex.
- Sixty percent of sexually transmitted diseases are transmitted when the partners are drunk.
- Forty percent of the men in one study thought it was acceptable behavior to force sex on a woman who was drunk.
- Ninety percent of all sexual assaults occur while one or both participants are under the influence of alcohol.

Rohypnol is commonly referred to as "the date rape drug." Rohypnol is usually slipped into the drink of an unknowing victim. Since it is a sedative, it has many effects on its victims. It can cause muscle relaxation, slower psychomotor responses, and lower inhibitions. If Rohypnol is combined with alcohol or given in high doses, it can have an even worse effect. It can cause complete blackouts combined with amnesia for eight to twelve hours. The effects from this drug can be felt within twenty to thirty minutes, with the strongest effects occurring within one to two hours. Rohypnol is illegal in the United States but can be obtained legally in sixty other countries, including Mexico and Latin America.

Another popular drug used in acquaintance rape is gamma hydroxybutrate (GHB), which is also known as Liquid Ecstasy and which is used in the same way as Rohypnol. GHB is in liquid form and has a very salty taste. It frequently is slipped into salty drinks like margaritas or other strong fruity drinks that can mask the taste. It is made from a combination of engine degreaser and lye.

Here are some tips to protect yourself from being inadvertently drugged:

- ☐ Never leave your drink unattended.
- ☐ Always keep your drink within sight.
- ☐ Be careful whom you accept drinks from. Do not take any beverages, including alcohol, from someone you do not know well and trust.
- ☐ While at a club or bar, accept drinks only from the bartender or wait staff.
- ☐ At parties, do not accept open-container drinks from anyone.
- ☐ Be sure you know the contents of your drink.
- ☐ Be alert to the behavior of your companions.
- ☐ If your companion appears inebriated, be concerned.
- ☐ If you believe you or someone else has consumed Rohypnol or any other drug, call 911 or go to the emergency room promptly.

Be careful and look out for yourself and your friends!

(Sources: American College Health Association, "Acquaintance Rape: What Everyone Should Know," <http://www.acha.org>; The University of Georgia Health Center, "A Parents' and Students' Guide for Understanding Acquaintance Rape," <http://www.uhs.uga.edu>; Drug Enforcement Agency, <http://www.usdoj.gov/dea/concern/ghb.htm>, <http://www.usdoj.gov /dea>; Date Rape Drugs, <http://www.mckinley.uiuc.edu/health-info/sexual /daterape/drape.html>; Date Rape Drug—Rohypnol, <http://www.4woman. gov/faq/rohypnol.htm>; "I Was a Victim of Date Rape," <http://www.uhs .uga.edu/sexwom-rape.html>; Sex and Alcohol, <http://www.uhs.uga.edu/ sexall-s&a.html>)

PART 4

THE EXTERNAL WORLD

14

TRAVEL SAFETY: HOW SAFE ARE YOU AS A TRAVELER?

 Travel safety relates to safety while driving, flying, and staying in hotel rooms and ensuring safety in a dangerous world. In all these situations, you must constantly be vigilant for your own personal security and for that of your fellow travelers. You should be aware of safety precautions in hotel rooms where you stay for business or leisure, and when driving your car at all times. These are important issues; however, in today's circumstances, it is important to discuss airline safety.

Airline Safety

Airline safety has become a topic of extreme importance since September 11. Having been the victim of an airline disaster myself, I know the apprehension one feels when it is necessary to travel by air again. Many new procedures are being put in place by the government, airlines, and airports. However, it is important to preplan your trip carefully to handle your anxieties. Allow yourself plenty of time to prepare for the trip and to get to the airport. Also try to put yourself in as calm a frame of mind as possible. If you are apprehensive, talk with the airline authorities so that they can reassure you of everything they are doing to make your trip both comfortable and safe.

Passengers

Each passenger must assume new responsibility for his or her safety.

- ☐ Evaluate the trip to see if there are other ways to conduct business, for example, a conference call or teleconferencing.
- ☐ Organize yourself thoroughly in preparation for travel.
- ☐ Travel lightly, taking only the essentials. Have luggage clearly marked, with your itinerary inside.
- ☐ Check all luggage, except for your purse, medicine, briefcase, and computer.
- ☐ Dress appropriately in only natural fibers, low-heeled shoes, and minimum jewelry.
- ☐ Give your itinerary to your next of kin before traveling.
- ☐ Do not board the plane if you are concerned.
- ☐ Always carry a cell phone with a charged backup battery.
- ☐ Do not drink alcohol on airplanes.
- ☐ Carry a smoke mask.
- ☐ Check with the U.S. Department of State for travel advisories.

Packing

The Federal Aviation Administration (FAA) advises that you remember to pack smart and safe. Passengers cannot bring the following items on their person or in carry-on luggage:

- ☐ Knives of any length, composition, or description

☐ All cutting and puncturing instruments. This includes pocketknives, carpet knives and box cutters, ice picks, straight razors, metal scissors, metal nail files, and knitting needles.

☐ Corkscrews

☐ Athletic equipment that could be used as a weapon, such as baseball/softball bats, golf clubs, pool cues, ski poles, and hockey sticks

☐ Fireworks—signal flares, sparklers, or other explosives

☐ Flammable liquids or solids—fuel, paints, lighter refills, matches

☐ Caustic household items such as drain cleaners and solvents

☐ Pressure containers—spray cans, butane fuel, scuba tanks, propane tanks, CO_2 cartridges, and self-inflating rafts

☐ Weapons—firearms, ammunition, gunpowder, mace, tear gas, or pepper spray

☐ Other hazardous materials—dry ice, gasoline-powered tools, wet-cell batteries, camping equipment with fuel, radioactive materials (except limited quantities), poisons, and infectious substances

Beware. Many common items used every day in the home or workplace may seem harmless. However, when transported by air, they can be very dangerous. In flight, variations in temperature and pressure can cause items to leak, generate toxic fumes, or start a fire.

Personal care items containing hazardous materials (for example, flammable perfume and aerosols) totaling no more than seventy ounces may be carried aboard. Contents of each container may not exceed sixteen fluid ounces.

Matches and lighters may only be carried on your person. However, "strike-anywhere" matches, lighters with flammable liquid reservoirs, and lighter fluid are forbidden.

A passenger on an aircraft may not carry firearms and ammunition. However, unloaded firearms may be transported in checked baggage if declared to the agent at check-in and packed in a suitable container. Handguns must be in a locked container. Boxed small-arms ammunition for personal use may be transported in checked luggage. Amounts may vary depending on the airline.

Dry ice (four pounds or less) for packing perishables may be carried on board an aircraft, provided the package is vented.

Electric wheelchairs must be transported in accordance with airline requirements. The battery may need to be disconnected and/or removed, and the terminals may need to be insulated to prevent short circuits.

Leave gifts unwrapped. Airline security personnel will open gifts if the X-ray scan cannot determine the contents.

If in doubt, don't pack it.

Do not travel if you are ill.

Arriving at the Airport

- ☐ Arrive early. Heightened airport security measures increase the time needed to check in. Arriving at the airport two hours before your flight's scheduled departure is advisable. Passengers may want to consult with their airline for more specific arrival times. Build in even more time at the airport if traveling with young children, infants, or passengers with disabilities.

- ☐ If you are using airport parking, give yourself plenty of time to find a secure parking place. Consider taking public transportation to the airport, if possible. Parking and curbside access will be controlled and limited.

- ☐ Curbside check-in is available only at specific locations. Contact your airline to see if it is available for your flight.

- ☐ Do not leave your car unattended in front of the terminal. Security measures dictate that unattended cars will be towed.

At the Airport

- ☐ Watch your bags and personal belongings at all times.
- ☐ Do not accept packages from strangers.
- ☐ If you see unattended bags or packages anywhere in the airport terminal or parking area, immediately report them to a security officer or other person of authority.
- ☐ Report any suspicious activities or individuals in the airport or parking lot to airport security.
- ☐ Don't joke about having a bomb or firearm. Don't discuss terrorism, weapons, explosives, or other threats while going through the security checkpoint. The mere mention of words such as "gun," "bomb," and so forth can compel security personnel to detain and question you. They are trained to consider these comments as real threats.

Checking In

- ☐ Adult passengers must bring a government-issued photo ID. The FAA requires that air carriers request government-issued identification, such as a driver's license or a passport, if the passenger appears old enough to have an ID. If a government-issued photo ID is not available, bring two pieces of ID, one of which must be from a governmental authority.
- ☐ E-ticket travelers should check with their airline to make sure they have proper documentation.
- ☐ Automated kiosks are available for airlines that have appropriate security measures in place. Travelers interested in this option should check with their airlines.
- ☐ Be prepared to answer questions about your bags. When asked who packed your bags and if you might have left them unattended at any time, think carefully and answer

the questions honestly. Criminals may use unsuspecting passengers to carry bombs or other dangerous items onto aircraft.

☐ Be cooperative as screeners ask to hand-search your bags. Security personnel will search a bag if the X-ray scan cannot determine its contents.

Screener Checkpoints

☐ Only ticketed passengers are allowed beyond the screener checkpoints, unless a passenger requires parental oversight or must be accompanied by a medical assistant.

☐ Travelers are limited to one carry-on bag and one personal item, for example, a purse or briefcase.

☐ Electronic items, such as laptop computers and cell phones, may be subjected to additional screening. Be prepared to remove your laptop from its travel case so it can be X-rayed separately.

On the Airplane

☐ Listen carefully to the flight attendant's safety instructions.

☐ Note where the exit closest to your seat is located.

☐ Wear your seat belt.

☐ Report unattended items to your flight attendant.

Hotel Safety

Traveling can be a wonderful opportunity to leave your troubles behind and relax. Although hotels do their best to assure a safe stay for their guests, it is a good idea to follow simple precautions to avoid problems.

General Tips

- ☐ Review hotel fire escape procedures and locate emergency exits, especially the closest one to your room, as you walk to your room. Many hotels have an emergency exit map located on the back of the room door.
- ☐ When checking in, women should use only their first initials and last names. Make sure the hotel clerk does not announce your room number. If it happens, request a new room.
- ☐ Use a hotel safe-deposit box for valuables, traveler checks, and cash you've brought with you. It is advisable not to bring valuable items with you when traveling.

Room Safety

- ☐ Never leave your room key or card unattended. If visiting the pool or fitness center, leave your room key at the front desk.
- ☐ If you lose your room key, contact the front desk immediately.
- ☐ As you approach your room, have your room key handy for quick entry.
- ☐ Always lock the door behind you.
- ☐ If you find the door to your room is ajar, do not enter. Contact the front desk.
- ☐ Leave on a light, television, or radio when leaving your room.
- ☐ Use all locks and chains on doors and windows while in the room.
- ☐ Use the peephole to identify callers.
- ☐ Refrain from opening the door if you are not expecting someone or you don't recognize the caller.

- [ ] If your room has a door that leads into another room, make sure it is locked.
- [ ] Don't hesitate to ask for employee identification from hotel personnel.
- [ ] Refuse deliveries that weren't requested and ask that they be left at the front desk.
- [ ] Don't leave your door open when carrying baggage in or out or using vending machines.
- [ ] Don't give your hotel number to strangers. Do not invite strangers to your room.
- [ ] Lock all luggage when you leave your room.

Personal Safety outside the Room

- [ ] Keep only change or small bills with you for taxis, small purchases, and tips.
- [ ] If you bring valuables, keep them hidden on your person.
- [ ] If you carry a handbag, keep it closed under your arm, with the strap on your shoulder.
- [ ] Put your wallet in your side pocket.
- [ ] Avoid carrying excess jewelry or expensive luggage.
- [ ] Consult with the concierge or front desk for detailed information about the city.
- [ ] Request to be escorted to your room if you prefer not walking alone.
- [ ] If you return to your room at night, use the hotel's main entrance.

Hotel Safety with Children

When traveling with your children, there are additional precautions you can take to have a safe stay.

☐ Check the room for safety hazards such as furniture with sharp corners, electrical outlets, loose equipment. Ask if the hotel offers a childproofing kit.

☐ Move all furniture away from windows.

☐ Tell children not to jump on the beds or stand on chairs.

☐ Put all hotel soaps, shampoos, bags, matches, and dry cleaning bags out of reach.

☐ Ensure that young children cannot reach glasses, coffeemakers, hair dryers, irons, or ironing boards.

☐ Keep a small light on during the night in case a child wakes and is confused.

☐ Don't leave children unsupervised at any time in the room.

☐ Place suitcases on the floor rather than on unstable suitcase racks.

☐ Ensure the television is out of reach of small children and can't be toppled if pulled.

☐ Check on the hot water for the bath before children turn on the tap. Hotels have a centralized boiler room and often have very hot water.

Following these simple safety tips can make your vacation trouble free and relaxing.

15

Weather Safety: How to Survive Mother Nature

A thirty-four-year-old little league coach was killed by a lightning strike while on the field.

During a recent tornado, seventeen people sought shelter under a highway overpass. All but one were blown out by the wind. One person was killed, one dismembered, and a dozen others suffered serious injuries.

 Weather can have devastating effects both on individuals and on property. Different types of weather conditions may require different precautions before and during an emergency. It is extremely important to know what disasters strike in the area where you live or travel, as there are several things you need to know to protect both yourself and your family.

Weather disasters include tornadoes, earthquakes, hurricanes, floods, lightning, droughts, heat waves, hurricanes, thunderstorms, volcanoes, and winter storms.

It is extremely important that you listen to the radio or television on a regular basis so that you know of an immediate weather threat to your area. It is also very important that you have a family plan and emergency supplies and that you heed all weather watches and warnings.

☐   Heed all weather warnings.
☐   Have a preplanned family survival plan.
☐   Practice the family plan.
☐   Have preassembled emergency disaster supplies.
☐   Have an emergency communication plan for your family.
☐   Buy a NOAA (National Oceanic and Atmospheric Administration) weather radio.
☐   For more information, see the websites <http://www.noaa.gov> and <http://www.fema.gov>.

Thunderstorms

Some thunderstorms can be seen approaching, while others hit without warning. It is important to learn and recognize the danger signs and to plan ahead.

Before a Thunderstorm

Learn the thunderstorm danger signs:

- Dark, towering, or threatening clouds
- Distant lightning and thunder

Have disaster supplies:

☐   Flashlight with extra batteries
☐   Portable, battery-operated radio with extra batteries

- ☐ First aid kit and manual
- ☐ Emergency food and water
- ☐ Nonelectric can opener
- ☐ Essential medicines
- ☐ Cash and credit cards
- ☐ Sturdy shoes

Check for yard hazards. Dead or rotting trees and branches can fall during a severe thunderstorm and cause injury and damage. Make sure all family members know how to respond after a thunderstorm. Teach family members how and when to turn off gas, electricity, and water. Teach children how and when to call 911, police, and the fire department. Make sure all members of your family know which radio station to tune to for emergency information.

Monitor severe thunderstorm watches and warnings. A severe thunderstorm watch is issued by the National Weather Service when the weather conditions are such that a severe thunderstorm is likely to develop.

A severe thunderstorm warning is issued when a severe thunderstorm has been sighted or indicated by weather radar. At this point, the danger is very serious and everyone should go to a safe place, turn on a battery-operated radio or television, and wait for the "all clear" announcement by the authorities.

Develop an emergency communication plan. In case family members are separated from one another during a thunderstorm, have a plan for getting back together. Ask an out-of-state relative or friend to serve as the "family contact."

During a Thunderstorm

If you are indoors:

- ☐ Secure outdoor objects such as lawn furniture that could blow away or cause damage or injury. Take light objects inside.

☐ Shutter windows securely and brace outside doors.

☐ Listen to a battery-operated radio or television for the latest storm information.

☐ Do not handle any electrical equipment or telephones, because lightning could follow the wire. Televisions sets are particularly dangerous at these times.

☐ Avoid bathtubs, water faucets, and sinks because metal pipes can transmit electricity.

If you are outdoors:

☐ Attempt to get into a building or a car.

☐ If no structure is available, get to an open space and squat low to the ground as quickly as possible.

☐ Crouch with hands on knees.

☐ Avoid tall structures such as towers, tall trees, and fences.

☐ Stay away from natural lightning rods such as golf clubs, tractors, fishing rods, bicycles, or camping equipment.

☐ Stay away from rivers, lakes, or other bodies of water. If you are isolated in a prairie and you feel your hair stand on end (which indicates that lightning is about to strike), bend forward, putting your hands on your knees. Remove all metal objects. A position with feet together and crouching is recommended. Do not lie flat on the ground.

If you are inside a car:

☐ Pull safely onto the shoulder of the road away from any trees that could fall on your vehicle.

☐ Stay in the car and turn on the emergency flashers until the heavy rain subsides.

☐ Avoid flooded roadways.

Lightning

Lightning can be a fascinating spectacle to watch. However, many people underestimate just how dangerous lightning is. There are an estimated twenty-five million cloud-to-ground lightning flashes a year, just in the United States alone. Lightning kills an average of seventy-three people per year, while another three hundred people suffer from lightning injuries. There are very few people who really understand the dangers of lightning. People must protect their lives, property, and the lives of others promptly, because during a thunderstorm each flash of cloud-to-ground lightning is a potential killer. The determining factor depends on whether a person is in the path of a lightning discharge. Some of the victims are struck directly by the main lightning stroke, but many victims are struck as the current moves in and along the ground. Virtually all people take some protective actions during the most dangerous part of a thunderstorm. But many leave themselves vulnerable to being struck by lightning as thunderstorms approach, depart, or are nearby.

What to Look For

According to the American Red Cross, look for darkening skies, flashes of light, or increasing winds. If you can hear thunder, you are close enough to be struck by lightning. Lightning can strike as much as ten miles away from the rain area in a thunderstorm. Listen to NOAA Weather Radio for up-to-date weather information.

What to Do When a Storm Approaches

- ☐ Find shelter in a building or car.
- ☐ Keep the car windows closed and don't take refuge in a convertible.
- ☐ Unplug appliances, including telephone lines.
- ☐ Avoid taking a bath or shower or being near running water.

☐ Turn off the air conditioner.
☐ Draw blinds and shades over windows to protect against glass shattering into your home.
☐ Avoid contact with plumbing.
☐ Stay away from doors and windows, and stay off porches.
☐ Do not lie down on concrete floors, and do not lean against concrete walls.

What to Do If Caught Outside

☐ Go to a low-lying, open place away from trees, poles, or metal objects.
☐ Become as small a target as possible by squatting as low as possible to the ground.
☐ Do not lie flat on the ground.

What to Do If Someone Is Struck by Lightning

The human body doesn't carry an electrical charge, so people struck by lightning can be handled safely. Get someone to dial 911 or your local emergency medical services number. Check the body for burns from where the person was struck to where the electricity left the body. Give the person first aid. If breathing has stopped, begin rescue breathing. If the heart has stopped beating, a trained person should give CPR. If the person has a pulse and is breathing, locate and care for other possible injuries.

(Sources: Red Cross of America, <http://www.redcross.org>; National Weather Service, <http://www.noaa.gov>)

Hail

Hail is produced by many strong thunderstorms. Hail can be smaller than a pea or as large as a softball and can be very destructive to

plants and crops. In a hailstorm, take cover immediately.
(Source: Federal Emergency Management Administration, <http://www.fema.gov>)

Floods

Flash floods are the number one weather-related killer in the United States. The two key factors that cause flash floods are rainfall intensity and duration. Topography, soil conditions, and ground cover also play an important role. Flash floods occur within a few minutes or hours of excessive rainfall, a dam or levee failure, or a sudden release of water held by an ice jam, while regular floods can take days to develop. Most flood deaths result from flash floods. Floods can occur nationwide. Even six inches of fast-moving floodwater can knock you off your feet, and a depth of two feet will float your car. Nearly half of all flash flood fatalities are auto related. Flooding has caused the deaths of more than ten thousand people since 1990. Property damage from flooding now totals over $1 billion each year in the United States.

Before the Flood

- [ ] Know information such as your flood risk, your elevation above flood stage, and if your local streams or rivers flood easily.
- [ ] Keep your automobile fueled, just in case you need to evacuate.
- [ ] Store drinking water in clean bathtubs and in various containers.
- [ ] Keep a stock of food that requires little cooking and no refrigeration.
- [ ] Have first aid supplies, a NOAA weather radio, a battery-powered portable radio, emergency cooking equipment, and flashlights on hand.

☐ Check to see if you have insurance that covers flooding. If not, find out how to get flood insurance. Keep insurance policies, documents, and other valuables in a safe-deposit box.

During the Flood

If you are advised to evacuate, do so immediately. Move to a safe area before access is cut off by floodwater, and monitor NOAA Weather Radio, television, and an emergency broadcast station for information.

Avoid areas subject to sudden flooding. If you come upon a flowing stream where water is above your ankles, stop, turn around, and go another way. Never attempt to drive over a flooded road. The depth of the water is not always obvious. The roadbed may be washed out under the water, and you could be stranded or trapped.

After the Flood

What should you do if you have been the victim of a flood? It is important to ensure safe drinking water, food, electricity, and sanitation. Read the following tips.

General Tips

☐ Food, clothing, shelter, and first aid are available from the Red Cross.

☐ Do not visit the disaster area, because your presence might hamper rescue and other emergency operations.

☐ Electrical equipment should be checked and dried before being returned to service.

☐ Use flashlights, not lanterns, torches, or matches, to examine buildings.

☐ Report broken utility lines to appropriate authorities.

☐ If your home is flooded, be sure utilities are off. Don't turn them on until notified.

☐ Avoid weakened structures, particularly floors, walls, and rooftops.

☐ Do not pump your basement out until floodwater recedes.

Drinking Water

If your well has been flooded, assume the water in your home has been contaminated. If you are on public water, your local health jurisdiction will let you know, through local media, if your water is not safe to drink. Bottled water is the best choice. If you can, get commercially bottled water that has been stored for less than six months in tightly sealed containers. Plan for one gallon per person per day.

☐ If the fresh drinking water supply has come in contact with floodwaters, throw it out.

☐ Boil drinking water before using it. Seek necessary medical care at the nearest hospital.

Cleanup/ Hygiene

☐ Wash your hands often, using soap and disinfected water.

☐ Make sure hands are washed when preparing or eating food, after using the toilet, and during and after handling contaminated items in flood cleanup activities.

☐ Wear gloves and boots.

☐ Do not touch anything with bare hands. Be careful not to step on glass.

Food

☐ Throw out fresh or frozen food that has come into contact with floodwater.

☐ Throw out food that has not been properly refrigerated.

☐ Undamaged canned goods are safe, but before opening, disinfect cans in a dilute bleach solution.

Electronics

Do not use electrical appliances that have been wet. Water can damage the motors in electrical appliances such as furnaces, freezers, refrigerators, washing machines, and dryers. If electrical appliances have been under water, have them dried out and reconditioned by a qualified service repairman. Use a ground fault circuit interrupter (GCFI) to help prevent electrocutions and electrical shock injuries.

Tornadoes

With tornadoes you have a very short time to make a life or death decision. Advance planning and quick responses are key to your survival. A tornado is defined as a violently rotating column of air extending from a thunderstorm to the ground. The most violent tornadoes are capable of tremendous destruction, with wind speeds of 250 miles per hour or more. Damage paths can be in excess of one mile wide and fifty miles long. According to the NOAA, in an average year eight hundred tornadoes are reported nationwide.

The Basics

The tornado is one of the most destructive forces in nature. With winds that can approach three hundred miles per hour, tornadoes can cause extensive devastation. It is important to know what to look for, when they occur, and how to react.

What to Look For

According to the NOAA, tornadoes often form when the following conditions are present: a dark, often greenish sky, large hail, a wall cloud, and a loud roar, similar to a freight train. Some tornadoes appear as a visible funnel extending only partially to the ground. Look for signs of debris below the visible funnel. Some tornadoes are clearly visible, while others are obscured by rain or nearby low-hanging clouds.

When Are Tornadoes Most Likely to Occur?

They can happen any time of the year and any time of day. They are most likely to occur between 3 P.M. and 9 P.M. In the southern states, peak season is from March through May. In the northern states, peak times are during the summer.

Who Is Most at Risk during Tornadoes?

People in automobiles, people in mobile homes, the elderly, the very young, people with physical or mental impairments, or people who may not understand the warnings because of a language barrier.

Before Tornado Season

As with any disaster, ensuring adequate preparations before disaster strikes is the best policy. There are basic tips and preparations that should be followed to ensure your safety in case a tornado strikes.

Basic Tips

☐ Conduct tornado drills each tornado season.
☐ Designate an area in the home as a shelter.
☐ Practice having everyone in the family go to the designated area.
☐ Know the difference between a tornado watch and a tornado warning.
☐ Have disaster supplies on hand.

Emergency Disaster Kit

Put an emergency disaster kit together that is available to all members of the family. In addition to the supplies in the emergency supply kit, have these disaster supplies on hand:

☐ Flashlight and extra batteries

- ☐ Portable, battery-operated radio and extra batteries
- ☐ First aid kit and manual
- ☐ Emergency food and water
- ☐ Nonelectric can opener
- ☐ Essential medicines
- ☐ Cash and credit cards, and your personal ID
- ☐ Sturdy shoes
- ☐ Blankets
- ☐ Bike helmet for your head

How to Prepare Ahead of Time

Stay tuned to weather forecasts for the most current information, watches, and warnings. Have a NOAA weather radio with a warning alarm tone and a battery backup. These radios will sound an alarm when there is a tornado, a watch, or a warning, even when you are sleeping. You should also develop a plan for you and your family, so that you know where to take shelter at home, at work, at school, or when outdoors.

How to Protect Yourself during a Tornado

Move to a predesignated shelter such as a basement in a home or building. If an underground shelter is not available, move to an interior room or hallway on the lowest floor and get under a sturdy piece of furniture. If you have a bike helmet, put it on your head to avoid injury from flying debris. Stay away from windows, get out of cars, do not try to outpace a tornado. If you are outside, lie flat in a nearby ditch or depression.

Develop an Emergency Communication Plan

Have a plan so that all members of your family know how to contact each other if you should become separated. If you are apart, have a family friend or relative who can be the central contact person. Make sure everyone knows the name, telephone number, and address of the contact person. This person should live out of the area, because you can often call long distance more easily than you can call locally in an emergency weather disaster.

Tornadoes and Tornado Warnings

Tornadoes can strike almost anywhere. They strike unexpectedly and often take people by surprise, which can result in a potentially more deadly situation. Tornadoes, however, can vary significantly in size, speed, and intensity. It is important to learn what tornadoes look like, how they are measured, and how weather forecasts distinguish between the possibility of a tornado and an imminent threat.

Tornado Watch

According to the Federal Emergency Management Agency, the National Weather Service issues a tornado watch when tornadoes are possible in your area. Remain alert for approaching storms. Remind all family members where the safest place is located and listen to the radio or television for further developments.

Tornado Warning

A tornado warning is issued when a tornado has been sighted or indicated by weather radar.

Tornado Danger Signs

- ☐ An approaching cloud of debris can mark the location of tornado even if a funnel is not visible.
- ☐ Before the tornado hits, the wind may die down and the air may become very still.
- ☐ Tornadoes generally occur near the trailing edge of a thunderstorm. Often, sunlit skies are behind a tornado.

Fugita-Pearson Tornado Scale

- ☐ F-0—40–72 mph—chimney damage, tree branches broken
- ☐ F-1—73–112 mph—mobile homes pushed off foundation or overturned

- [ ] F-2—113–157 mph—considerable damage, mobile homes demolished, trees uprooted
- [ ] F-3—158–205 mph—roofs and walls torn down, trains overturned, cars thrown
- [ ] F-4—207–260 mph—well-constructed walls leveled
- [ ] F-5—261–318 mph—homes lifted off foundation and carried considerable distances, autos thrown as far as 100 meters

During the Tornado

If at Home

- [ ] Go to a windowless, interior room; basement; or the lowest level of the building. If there is no basement, go to an inner hallway or a smaller inner room without windows, such as a closet.
- [ ] Get away from the windows.
- [ ] Go to the center of the room.
- [ ] Stay away from corners, because they tend to attract debris.
- [ ] Get under a piece of sturdy furniture, such as a workbench or a heavy table or desk, and hold on to it.
- [ ] Use arms to protect your head and neck.
- [ ] Wear a bike helmet.
- [ ] If in a mobile home, find shelter elsewhere.

If in School or at Work

- [ ] Go to the basement or to an inside hallway at the lowest level.
- [ ] Avoid places with widespan roofs such as auditoriums, cafeterias, large hallways, or shopping malls.
- [ ] Get under a piece of sturdy furniture such as a workbench, heavy table, or desk and hold on to it.
- [ ] Use arms to protect head and neck and put on a helmet.

If Outdoors

- ☐ If possible, get inside a building.
- ☐ If shelter is not available or there is no time to get indoors, lie in a ditch or low-lying area or crouch near a strong building.
- ☐ Be aware of the potential for flooding.
- ☐ Use arms to protect your head and neck, and wear a helmet.

If in a Car

- ☐ Never try to out-drive a tornado in a car or truck; your car can be lifted by the tornado and tossed in the air.
- ☐ Get out of the car immediately and take shelter in a nearby building.
- ☐ If there is no time to get indoors, get out of the car and lie in a ditch or low-lying area, away from the vehicle. Be aware of the potential for flooding.

After the Tornado

- ☐ Help injured or trapped persons.
- ☐ Give first aid, if appropriate. Do not try to move the seriously injured unless they are in immediate danger of further injury.
- ☐ Call for help.
- ☐ Turn on a radio or television to get the latest emergency information.
- ☐ Stay out of damaged buildings. Return home only when it is safe.
- ☐ Use the telephone for emergency calls.
- ☐ Clean up spilled medicines, household cleaners, or flammable liquids to prevent fire or toxic fumes.
- ☐ Take pictures of the damage, both to the house and its contents, for insurance purposes.

☐ Help your neighbors, if they are elderly, infants, disabled, or require special assistance.

Conclusion

For more information on tornadoes visit <http://www.fema.gov> or <http://www.noaa.gov>.

Hurricanes

Some areas of the country are more prone to hurricanes than others, so people are often unprepared. However, hurricanes are a clear threat that everyone should know about, as they might someday be traveling through a hurricane-prone area. A hurricane causes sea levels to rise above normal tidal heights, with giant wind-driven waves and strong, unpredictable currents. These are the storm's worst killers. Tornadoes spawned by hurricanes are extremely dangerous. When a hurricane approaches, listen for tornado watches and warnings and be ready to take immediate shelter.

Before a Hurricane Occurs

Know your property's elevation above mean sea level. Have a safe evacuation route planned and learn the storm history of your area.

Prepare a Personal Evacuation Plan

☐ Identify ahead of time where you could go if you are told to evacuate. Choose several places—a friend's home in another town, a motel, or a shelter.

☐ Keep handy the telephone numbers of these places as well as a road map of your locality. You might need to take alternative or unfamiliar routes if major roads are closed or clogged.

- [ ] Listen to NOAA Weather Radio or local radio and television stations for evacuation instructions. If advised to evacuate, do so immediately.
- [ ] Contact your out-of-area contact to inform them of your plans.

Assemble a Disaster Supply Kit

- [ ] First aid kit and essential medications
- [ ] Canned food and can opener
- [ ] At least three gallons of water per person
- [ ] Protective clothing, rainwear, and bedding or sleeping bags
- [ ] Battery-powered radio, flashlight, and extra batteries
- [ ] Special items for infants, elderly, or disabled family members
- [ ] Written instructions on how to turn off electricity, gas, and water if authorities advise you to do so

Hurricane Watch

Hurricane conditions may pose a threat to your area. In especially vulnerable areas, early evacuation may be necessary when a watch is issued. Otherwise you should review hurricane safety procedures and make preparations. Listen to NOAA Weather Radio and commercial radio and television for the latest information and instructions for your location. Prepare to bring inside any lawn furniture, outdoor decorations or ornaments, trash cans, hanging plants, and anything else that can be picked up by the wind. Prepare to cover all windows of your home. If shutters have not been installed, use precut plywood. Make sure your car has a full gas tank. Recheck manufactured home tie-downs. Check batteries and stock up on canned foods, first aid supplies, drinking water, and medications.

Hurricane Warning

When hurricane conditions are expected in your area within twenty-four hours, areas subject to storm surge or tides should be evacuated as well as areas that could be isolated by floodwaters. Follow the instructions of local officials. You will not be asked to leave your home unless your life is threatened. Complete preparation activities. If out on the water, moor your boat securely or evacuate it. If you are advised not to evacuate your home, stay indoors, away from windows. Be aware that the calm "eye" is deceptive and the storm is not over. Be alert for tornadoes, because they can occur during and after a hurricane. Remain indoors, in the center of your home, in a closet or bathroom without windows. Stay away from floodwaters.

Latest storm-related information will be available on NOAA Weather Radio and commercial radio and television.

Know What to Do after a Hurricane Is Over

Keep listening to NOAA Weather Radio or local radio and television stations for instructions. If you are evacuated, return home when local officials tell you it is safe to do so. Inspect your home for damage and use flashlights instead of candles in the dark.

(Sources: National Weather Service, <http://www.nws.nooa.gov>; Red Cross, <http://www.redcross.org>)

Earthquakes

Earthquakes strike suddenly, violently, and without warning. Identifying potential hazards and making plans in advance can reduce the chances of serious injury or loss of life.

Before an Earthquake

To protect yourself in the event of an earthquake, make adequate preparations before an earthquake occurs. Eliminate hazards, develop an earthquake emergency plan with family members, and prepare a disaster supply kit.

Eliminating Hazards

- ☐ Bolt bookcases, china cabinets, and other tall furniture to wall studs.
- ☐ Install strong latches on cupboards and strap the water heater to wall studs.
- ☐ Place large or heavy objects on lower shelves.
- ☐ Store breakable items such as bottled foods, glass, and china in low, closed cabinets with latches.
- ☐ Hang heavy items such as pictures and mirrors away from beds, couches, and where people sit.
- ☐ Brace overhead light fixtures. Repair defective electrical wiring and leaky gas connections. These are potential fire risks.
- ☐ Secure a water heater by strapping it to the wall studs and bolting it to the floor.
- ☐ Repair any deep cracks in ceilings or foundations.
- ☐ Store weed killers, pesticides, and flammable products securely in closed cabinets with latches and on bottom shelves.
- ☐ Get expert advice if there are signs of structural defects.

Family Members

Teach all family members how and when to turn off gas, electrical current, and water. Teach children when and how to call 911, the police, and the fire department, and which radio station to tune to for emergency information. Ask an out-of-state relative or friend to serve as the family contact. After a disaster, it's often easier to call long distance. Develop an emergency communication plan. In case family members are separated from one another during an earthquake, which is a real possibility during the day when adults are at work and children are at school, develop a plan for reuniting after the disaster.

Disaster Supplies
- ☐ Flashlights
- ☐ Portable battery-operated radio and extra batteries
- ☐ First aid kit and manual
- ☐ Emergency food and water
- ☐ Nonelectric can opener
- ☐ Essential medicines
- ☐ Cash and credit cards
- ☐ Sturdy shoes

During an Earthquake

Earthquakes are always frightening and have the potential to cause significant damage. You can help improve your safety and that of your loved ones by following these steps.

Indoor Safety during an Earthquake
Take cover under a piece of heavy furniture or against an inside wall and hold on. Stay inside and away from the glass that could shatter around windows, mirrors, and pictures. The most dangerous thing to do during the shaking of an earthquake is to try to leave the building, because objects can fall on you.

Outdoor Safety during an Earthquake
Move into the open, away from buildings, streetlights, and utility wires. Once in the open, stay there until the shaking stops.

Moving Vehicle Safety during an Earthquake

Stop quickly and stay in the vehicle. Move to a clear area away from buildings, trees, overpasses, or utility wires. Once the shaking has stopped, proceed with caution. Avoid bridges or ramps that might have been damaged by the quake.

After the Earthquake

After an earthquake, the tasks of rescue and recovery begin. Most importantly, immediate action is required to make sure that family, friends, and neighbors are all right. These efforts must be undertaken while guarding against aftershocks, gas leaks, electrical shorts, and sewage seepage.

Immediate Action

Help injured or trapped persons. Give first aid where appropriate. Do not move seriously injured persons unless they are in immediate danger of further injury. Call for help.

Listen to a battery-operated radio or television for the latest emergency information. Remember neighbors who may require special assistance—infants, the elderly, and people with disabilities.

Stay out of damaged buildings. Only return home when authorities say it is safe. Use the telephone only for emergency calls. Clean up spilled medicines, bleaches, or gasoline and other flammable liquids immediately. Leave the area if you smell gas or fumes from other chemicals. Open closet and cupboard doors with caution. Inspect the entire length of chimneys carefully for damage. Unnoticed damage could lead to a fire.

Pets after an Earthquake

The behavior of pets may change dramatically after an earthquake. Normally quiet and friendly cats and dogs may become aggressive or defensive. Watch animals closely. Leash dogs and place them in a fenced yard. Pets may not be allowed into shelters for health and space reasons. Prepare an emergency pen for pets in the home that includes a three-day supply of dry food and a large container of water.

Aftershocks

Although smaller than the main shock, aftershocks cause additional damage and may bring weakened structures down. Aftershocks can occur in the first hours, days, weeks, or even months after the quake.

If Damage Has Occurred

Gas Leaks

If you smell gas or hear a blowing or hissing noise, open a window and quickly leave the building. Turn off the gas at the outside main valve if you can and call the gas company from a neighbor's home. If you turn off the gas for any reason, a professional must turn it back on.

Electrical System

If you see sparks or broken or frayed wires, or if you smell hot insulation, turn off the electricity at the main fuse box or circuit breaker, but call an electrician first for advice.

Sewage

If you suspect sewage lines are damaged, avoid using toilets and call a plumber. If water pipes are damaged, contact the water company and avoid using water from the tap. You can obtain safe water by melting ice cubes.

(Sources: American Red Cross, <http://www.redcross.org>; Federal Emergency Management Agency, <http://www.fema.gov>)

16

MEDICAL EMERGENCIES
AND SAFETY:
HOW TO RESPOND

A man in his sixties was in the hospital for routine treatment when an overdose of a prescription medicine permanently damaged his liver.

A child underwent minor surgery at a children's hospital. She was given the wrong prescription medicine and died.

A woman was having a gallbladder attack and the emergency room of the local hospital recommended a doctor to remove the gallbladder. Upon further research, it was discovered that the doctor was unqualified and uncertified in the state. She canceled the surgery with that doctor and found a qualified, certified physician.

First Aid

 In a world where tragedy can strike anyone at any time, first aid is a skill that everyone should have. From reading this book, it is apparent that danger lurks everywhere. Countless lives could be saved, and the severity of many injuries would be reduced, if only people learned about how to administer first aid. Many of us learned about first aid when we were in school or at summer camp. Sadly, most of us have probably forgotten what we learned.

One organization that has a long tradition of teaching first aid and helping to deal with health issues is the Red Cross. This organization is a great resource and has classes that teach how to administer different forms of first aid.

The following section details appropriate first aid techniques for a variety of injuries and accidents.

Mouth-to-Mouth Resuscitation

Mouth-to-mouth resuscitation is necessary for casualties in complete respiratory arrest. Choking, heroin overdose, near drowning, and certain bites and stings, as well as respiratory conditions such as asthma and emphysema, can cause respiratory arrest, necessitating rapid and effective action. Mouth-to-mouth resuscitation is the method by which a rescuer breathes for a victim who has stopped breathing. There are three main methods for delivering resuscitation:

- Mouth-to-mouth: The rescuer seals the victim's mouth with his or her mouth and breathes into the airway through the mouth.
- Mouth-to-nose: This technique is used when the victim has sustained facial injuries that preclude using the mouth. The first aid worker closes the victim's mouth, seals the nose with

his or her mouth, breathes gently, then releases the victim's jaw to allow the victim to exhale.

- Mouth-to-nose-and-mouth is the best method to use when resuscitating a child because the rescuer's mouth can cover and seal the child's nose and mouth.

Although instructions for administering mouth-to-mouth resuscitation are given below, it is strongly recommended that all readers of this book go to their local Red Cross, fire or police department, or hospital to learn firsthand how to perform this technique.

☐ Roll victim away from you and check airway.
☐ Place victim on back and open airway.
☐ Look, listen, and feel for breathing.
☐ Place mouth over victim's mouth or nose and give five breaths.
☐ Assess the victim's breathing status and check for pulse.
☐ Continue effort by giving one full breath every four seconds, or fifteen breaths per minute.
☐ For children and infants, give one full breath every three seconds, or twenty breaths per minute.
☐ Reassess airway and pulse after one minute and then every two minutes.

Full breaths should be used only for an adult victim. For children, ensure that you modify the force of the breaths. If the breaths are delivered too forcefully, the child could vomit.

The method that should be used for infants and very young children is to fill your mouth with air and puff it into the child's mouth.

Resuscitation should be continued until the victim begins breathing spontaneously, until the rescuer is relieved by medical aid, or until the victim deteriorates into full cardiac arrest, at which point cardiopulmonary resuscitation needs to be used.

Cardiopulmonary Resuscitation

Cardiopulmonary resuscitation (CPR) is the most effective form of resuscitation and is used to revive the beating of the victim's heart and can sustain the victim until expert medical treatment is available.

To administer CPR properly, the rescuer's hands should be positioned correctly in relation to the victim's heart. To locate the correct position for the hands, two fingers should be placed over the small bump at the base of the victim's sternum, and then the hand should be placed centrally on the chest, above the two fingers. This position should be near the heart. The second hand is placed over the first, and the fingers are entwined for stability. Compressions are performed at a depth of about one inch, using the heel of one hand only. You should be careful not to damage the ribcage.

An infant's heart should be located by placing two fingers centrally on the lower half of the sternum. Compressions are performed by pressing with the fingers one inch deep. Because a child's chest is smaller, you should modify the pressure you use. The pulse is detected by placing a finger directly over the left nipple.

Although instructions for administering cardiopulmonary resuscitation are given below, it is strongly recommended that all readers of this book go to their local Red Cross, fire or police department, or hospital to learn firsthand how to perform this technique.

Procedure for One-Person CPR

- ☐ Check for response by shaking and shouting at the victim.
- ☐ Roll the victim away from you and check and clear the airway.
- ☐ Place the victim on the back on a firm, flat surface and open his or her airway.
- ☐ Look, listen, and feel for breathing.
- ☐ Give five quick breaths.
- ☐ Assess the status of breathing by looking at the diaphragm.

- ☐ Check for a pulse at the neck for about five seconds.
- ☐ Kneel beside victim's chest and locate his or her heart on the lower half of chest.
- ☐ Place your hands centrally over heart, with fingers entwined.
- ☐ Lean over the victim with your arms straight and elbows locked.
- ☐ Commence 15 compressions, with even pressure until resistance is felt, with a compression rate of 60 to 80 compressions per minute for adults, and 80 to 100 compressions per minute for children and infants.
- ☐ Give two breaths.
- ☐ Relocate the heart.
- ☐ Give 15 compressions.
- ☐ Repeat the cycle for one minute and then check for a pulse in the neck.
- ☐ Continue the cycle for two minutes and then check for a pulse in the neck.
- ☐ Continue the cycle and recheck the pulse every two minutes.

CPR should be continued until either the victim is revived, you are relieved by expert medical aid, or you are too exhausted to continue. If the victim regains consciousness, lay him or her on his or her side and observe closely.

Abrasions and Injuries

You should know how to treat wounds safely to prevent infection, to keep them clean, and to facilitate healing. Injuries can include incisions, lacerations, abrasions, and puncture wounds. Follow these instructions to treat them.

- ☐ Examine the wound but do not remove any penetrating object.

☐   Clean the wound and use an antiseptic solution, if necessary.

☐   Apply pressure to stop any bleeding.

☐   Place a bandage over the wound and apply a roller bandage, if necessary.

☐   Rest and raise the injured limb, if possible.

Burns, Blisters, and Scalds

Burns are caused by contact with flame, hot objects, chemicals, electrocution, radiated heat, or frozen surfaces, while scalds are caused by contact with boiling fluids or steam. As with most potentially serious injuries, prevention is better than cure.

Burns are classified as either superficial, in which the skin is reddened and blisters appear, or deep, in which there is destruction of tissue and nerves and a whitish or blackened area surrounded by superficial burns. For deep burns, call 911. For superficial burns and blisters, read and follow the first aid instructions below.

General Treatment for Burns and Blisters

☐   Cool with water—ten minutes for heat burns or twenty minutes for chemical burns.

☐   Cover with a clean bandage.

☐   Call for an ambulance if the burn is severe.

☐   Do not overcool, because it could cause shivering.

☐   Do not use creams or ointments unless prescribed.

☐   Do not attempt to remove material associated with the burn.

Blisters

You can prevent some blisters from forming by covering the area with several layers of sterile gauze at the first sign of discomfort. In the event of a blister, do the following things:

☐ Sterilize a needle by holding it for ten seconds in a flame.

☐ Puncture the edge of the blister, next to the skin.

☐ Apply gentle pressure, squeezing the accumulated fluid out of the blister. Make sure not to peel back or brush off the skin that formed over the blister, because it guards against infection.

☐ Treat the blister with either antibiotic ointment or rubbing alcohol and cover with several layers of sterile gauze.

Burns

Burns are quite serious for adults and even more serious and harmful to children. Even hot tap water can cause a third-degree burn on a child. Burns fall into two categories—scalds and contact burns. Hot liquids or steam cause incidents of scalding, while touching hot objects causes burns. You should attempt first aid treatment only for first-degree burns in which the skin is reddened and slightly swollen.

If you receive a second- or third-degree burn in which the skin is blistered or charred, or that covers a large area of skin, you should seek medical treatment immediately.

☐ For a first-degree burn, immediately immerse the burn in cold water and keep it immersed until you no longer feel pain. If necessary, periodically add ice cubes to the water to keep it cold. Do not put butter or any other greasy product on the burn.

☐ Apply one of the following to the burn: a commercial burn ointment, a thick layer of honey, or a thick paste of baking soda and water.

☐ Cover the burn with a loose protective bandage that allows some exposure to air.

Chemical Burns

- ☐ Flush the burned area with plenty of running cold water to remove traces of the chemical.
- ☐ Apply either a burn ointment, a thick layer of honey or petroleum jelly, or a thick paste of baking soda and water to the burned area.
- ☐ Cover with a loose protective bandage.
- ☐ If the chemical burn involves the eye, immediately flush the eye with plenty of running water, cover it with a sterile pad to keep the lid still, and contact medical help immediately.

Choking

Children are most at risk of choking and children under the age of three are the most at-risk age group of children for choking. Although food causes the majority of choking incidents, according to Safe Kids, five thousand children under the age of fourteen have to visit the hospital after choking on toys. Balloons, pennies, peanuts, and other foods such as hot dogs, candy, grapes, popcorn, and carrots are the most common culprits in incidents of choking.

To prevent choking, you should follow these tips:

- ☐ Keep small objects out of the reach of children.
- ☐ Inspect toys for damage regularly.
- ☐ Tie up window and other types of cords, cut the ends, or use safety tassels.
- ☐ Remove drawstrings from clothing.
- ☐ Never allow children to wear scarves, necklaces, or purses on playground equipment.
- ☐ When purchasing new toys, always refer to the age label.
- ☐ Purchase a testing device that can be used to test small objects to see if they are choking hazards.

☐ Refer to the chapters on home, food, clothing, toy, and playground safety.

If a person who is choking is coughing effectively, do not slap him or her on the back. If the obstruction is at the entrance to the trachea, the slaps may cause complete obstruction. If the victim initially coughs to no effect and appears to be in increasing distress, then the object may be totally obstructing the airway.

To treat the victim, take the following actions: position the victim—adults laterally, children heads down—and deliver three or four firm slaps between the shoulder blades. Then reassess the victim's attempts to breathe and repeat three or four firm slaps.

If this fails to free the object and the victim has collapsed, quickly roll the victim onto his or her side, place your hands over the ribs, and deliver quick, firm thrusts. This may expel the object through the forcing of residual air from the lungs. Alternate slaps and chest thrusts. If this is not effective and the victim is in respiratory arrest, begin mouth-to-mouth resuscitation immediately.

Drowning

Drowning is one of the greatest threats to children, regardless of age. Buckets, bathtubs, the toilet, and any other thing that contains water is a serious threat to a child. If your household has a swimming pool, a wading pool, or a whirlpool, or if there are any bodies of water near your house, adults must exercise great caution if children are around. Because drowning is so dangerous, prevention is the key. Follow these preventative steps to decrease the risk of someone drowning:

☐ Never leave your child alone in water, in the bathroom, or near buckets for any reason or for any length of time.
☐ The best line of defense against pool injuries or possible drowning is constant supervision. Drowning can happen

in a matter of seconds. There is no substitute for close supervision.

☐ Teach children not to get into the tub, a pool, a pond, or any other body of water without adult supervision.

☐ Never leave pails, buckets, or other containers with water around. Always empty containers of water when you are finished using them.

☐ Keep the bathroom door closed and always keep the toilet lid down.

☐ Do not rely on baby bathtub "supporting ring" devices to keep baby safe in the tub. Never leave a baby alone in these bath support rings. Even turning away to answer the doorbell or telephone can result in drowning or submersion of the baby.

To treat a near-drowning victim, perform mouth-to-mouth resuscitation and CPR, as necessary, call 911, and seek emergency medical attention.

Electric Shock

Electrical burns are difficult to detect. A person who has received a severe electrical shock may have badly burned underlying tissue, even though the surface skin shows little evidence of this. Get the victim prompt medical attention. Unattended electrical burns can lead to serious complications.

Someone who has sustained an electrical shock can be in an extremely critical state. Do not touch the victim if he or she is still touching the electrical equipment that caused the shock. The first step to handle the situation is to disconnect the electrical cord from the socket or turn off the building's electrical breakers or fuse box. If this isn't possible, separate the victim from the source of the electrical current with a long, dry stick, a dry rope, or a long dry cloth. Be sure that your hands are dry and that you are standing on a dry surface.

Once you have removed the person from the source of the contact, check to see if he or she is breathing. If not, begin mouth-to-mouth resuscitation immediately. If someone else is available, have him or her call the fire or police departments and/or the ambulance. You should continue mouth-to-mouth breathing until the ambulance arrives.

Heat and Cold

The human body maintains a body temperature of about 98.6 degrees Fahrenheit. Any excessive variation to this range affects the functions of the body. Generally, the brain does not react well to heat, and the heart is sensitive to cold. The body has some natural defense mechanisms against excessive heat and cold. It regulates body heat by sweating and other means. Cold is managed by shivering, which generates heat within the body. Environmental influences often determine the stability of the human body's temperature.

Heat-Related Illnesses

Heat-related conditions are conditions brought on by exposure to high temperatures and humidity. The following will help you treat illnesses related to heat:

Heat Cramps

When the body is losing more fluids than it is replacing, heat cramps result. This condition causes muscular contraction. Symptoms may include pale and cool skin, sweating, cramping pains in the limbs or abdomen, nausea, and spasms.

To treat the victim, take the following actions: Put at rest in the shade, give sips of cool water to drink, do not massage affected limb, and do not encourage further exercise.

Heat Exhaustion

Heat exhaustion is caused by exertion accompanied by heat and high humidity and particularly affects the very young and the elderly.

Symptoms may include fatigue, irritability, headache, faintness, weak but rapid pulse, shallow breathing, cool skin, and perspiration.

To treat, instruct the victim to lie down in a cool, shady area or air-conditioned room. Elevate his or her feet. Massage the legs toward the heart. Give cold salt water (a half teaspoon to half a glass of water) or cool, sweetened drinks, especially iced tea, every fifteen minutes until the victim recovers. Do not let the victim sit up, even after feeling recovered.

Heat Stroke

A heat stroke is potentially fatal. In this condition, the body's temperature regulation center in the brain has been rendered inoperable, and the temperature continually rises, causing eventual brain damage. Immediate active intervention is necessary to avoid coma and death. Symptoms may include extremely high body temperature (106 degrees Fahrenheit or higher); hot, red, dry skin; absence of sweating; rapid pulse; convulsions; and unconsciousness.

To treat, get professional medical help immediately. While waiting for help to arrive, try to lower the body temperature quickly by placing the victim in a partially filled tub of cool, not cold, water and place a sponge or damp cloth over the victim's body until his or her temperature is reduced, then dry with a towel. If a tub is not nearby, wrap the victim in cold, wet sheets in a well-ventilated room or use fans and air conditioners until the body temperature is reduced. Do not give stimulating beverages such as coffee, tea, or soda.

Sunburn

Apply cool cloths or lotion to the burned area to reduce pain and swelling, or give a cool shower. If the sunburn involves the victim's back or an area he or she can't reach, give the victim a bath in cool water. Dispense aspirin or other pain reliever to reduce the pain. Apply a thin paste of baking soda and water or calamine lotion to alleviate the pain. If blisters form, never break them. If blisters do break, apply an antibiotic ointment and cover the blisters with a sterile bandage. Although most sunburns are minor, the victim should seek medical help if the sunburn is severe, defined as one covering more than one fourth of the body or presenting extensive blistering.

Cold-Related Illnesses

Exposure to cold has effects that are no less serious than conditions caused by exposure to heat and humidity. An elderly person in an unheated house during winter, who is incapacitated and unable to summon assistance, is at risk from exposure to cold and hypothermia.

Frostbite

Frostbite initially looks like a reddened first-degree burn. A tingling sensation follows, ice crystals may form on the skin, and the skin will become yellowish-gray and feel numb.

Rewarm the frozen skin by submerging the affected body part in warm water. Do not rub the frozen skin to warm it with friction. When a reddish color returns to the frostbitten skin, take the affected body part out of the warm water and pat it dry gently. Take care not to break any blisters that may have formed and do not rub the skin. Cover the skin with a loose bandage and seek medical help immediately. If the feet or legs are frostbitten, do not let the victim attempt to walk.

Exposure

This common situation relates to persons suffering from low temperatures and usually is caused by being caught in inclement weather, by being soaked in cold water and unable to change, by being subjected to cold winds without proper protection, or simply by being elderly and not being able to afford proper heating and clothing. Symptoms include pale, cool skin, a slow, weak pulse, lethargy and drowsiness, lack of talking, and shivering.

To treat exposure to cold, you should take the following steps: Warm the victim slowly by adding additional clothing, a heating source and/or body heat. If the victim is wet, warm him or her, then change clothing and when partially recovered, give him/her a warm, sweet drink. When the victim is able to stand, encourage mild exercise.

Hypothermia

Hypothermia is a potentially fatal condition that especially affects the elderly. The body's core temperature has been lowered to the extent that the brain function is impaired and the heart's activity is about to be compromised. Urgent first aid intervention is required. Symptoms may include pale, cold skin, a slow pulse, breathing difficulties, blurred vision, and an absence of shivering. The victim also may become silent, appear to be asleep, and be difficult to rouse. If very cold, the victim may have nonreacting pupils and appear to be near death.

To treat, call for emergency services immediately. While waiting, warm the victim slowly by wrapping him or her in a blanket. If the victim is wet, leave less bulky clothing on and warm him or her slowly.

Strangulation

Clothing drawstrings, ribbons, cords, and other things cause many incidents of strangulation. Also, objects that are too small for the entire body of a child to fit through provide another type of risk and include items such as bunk beds, cribs, strollers, high chairs, and playground equipment. To prevent strangulation, follow the tips listed under choking and see the chapters on clothing and toy and playground safety. To treat a victim of strangulation, use mouth-to-mouth resuscitation and CPR.

Suffocation

Most suffocation, like strangulation and choking, occurs in the home. Children under three years old are at greatest risk for suffocation. Child suffocation can be attributed primarily to soft objects such as mattresses, pillows, or infant cushions as well as plastic bags or someone rolling over on top of a child. Children also can be trapped in household appliances such as the washer or dryer or in a toy chest. According to Safe Kids, cribs cause about fifty suffocation and strangulation deaths each year.

To treat a victim of suffocation, use mouth-to-mouth resuscitation and CPR.

By learning these first aid instructions, you know better how to treat a victim of an unintentional injury. If you, your loved ones, or anyone else falls victim to a hazard, whether it is choking, electrocution, poisoning, or a heat- or cold-related illness, knowing how to give effective first aid can make the difference between a serious injury and a not-so-serious one, or between life and death. Remember that prevention is by far the best way to ensure a safe environment in which first aid hopefully will never be necessary. Finally, it is strongly recommended that you take a first aid course and learn first aid procedure firsthand from qualified individuals.

Calling 911

The 911 emergency telephone system exists in many cities to facilitate responses to police, medical, or fire emergencies. I have no doubt that many lives have been saved because of 911. Most large cities and many smaller ones have 911 systems. If your city does not have this service, you should create a list of the appropriate emergency numbers and place it near each phone.

Although 911 has been an extremely valuable service, the number of inappropriate calls to the number has increased. For the record, 911 should not be called if you want to know the weather forecast, if you want to order a pizza, or if you want an answer to a trivial question. Nonemergency calls to the 911 system or any emergency phone number obstruct the handling of very serious emergencies that require immediate attention.

You should learn about the emergency systems in your hometown and wherever you may travel. The following are guidelines for the proper use of the 911 system for fire and medical emergencies for most major cities.

When to Use 911

Call 911 for emergencies requiring immediate attention, such as:

- Severe injuries from such things as traffic accidents, head injuries, significant falls, physical entrapment, and poisonings
- Breathing difficulty, shortness of breath, or situations where breathing has stopped, such as severe allergic reaction
- Sudden fainting and/or unconsciousness, especially when someone will not wake up even when you shake them
- Constant chest pain that lasts longer than two minutes
- Uncontrollable bleeding or large blood loss in situations where household appliances or tools have caused an injury or in the event of gunshot wounds or stabbing
- Instances of choking, drowning, electrocution, strangulation, poisoning, or drug overdose
- Severe reactions such as vomiting blood or undergoing convulsions or seizures
- Severe burns such as white or charred skin or blisters and redness over a large area

Nonemergency Situations

You should not call 911 for nonemergency situations. If you have one of the following problems, you should use the nonemergency numbers of your hospital, doctor, and so forth.

- Minor illnesses such as the flu or the common cold

- Instances of minor cuts, broken fingers or toes, or ongoing body aches and pains
- Emotional stress
- Routine transportation to medical offices, clinics, and hospitals

Calling 911: Placing the Call

When an emergency arises, you should go to the nearest telephone and dial 911. The first thing you must do is to identify the call as either a police, medical, or fire emergency. Often the dispatcher automatically will receive the address and telephone number of the caller. Once you identify the call, remember to remain calm. Even though you may be quite frantic, speak slowly and clearly. Give direct answers to the questions asked. You will be asked additional questions so the dispatcher can send the right type of help. All of the following questions are important.

☐ What's the emergency? What's wrong?
☐ Where is the emergency? Give the address, including building number and/or name, apartment number, and nearest cross street.
☐ Who needs help? Give the person's age and the number of victims.
☐ Tell the dispatcher whether the victim is conscious and/or breathing.

The dispatcher will verify the accuracy of all telephone numbers and addresses. The dispatcher also may provide you with critical pre-arrival instructions about emergency first aid such as CPR (cardiopulmonary resuscitation) or the Heimlich Maneuver. Once all the questions are answered and you have provided the necessary information, wait for the dispatcher to hang up before you do.

Understanding what happens when a 911 call is placed helps the system run more efficiently and brings the emergency care you need in the shortest possible time.

How to Help before Emergency Services Arrive

- ☐ Assure the patient that help is on the way.
- ☐ Do not tie up the telephone line after the 911 call is made.
- ☐ Direct someone to meet the ambulance and lead the way.
- ☐ Wave a flashlight or turn on car lights or a porch light if it's dark or visibility is poor.
- ☐ Ask for an interpreter if the patient does not speak English.
- ☐ Secure pets, especially dogs, in a separate area.
- ☐ Have a visible posted address, easily readable from the street.
- ☐ Make a list of medications the patient is using and give it to emergency personnel.

For more information contact your local American Red Cross chapter or your local hospital.

Patient Safety

People are very concerned today with various aspects of their family's safety, but they may overlook how safe they are as a patient or consumer of medical services. An estimated ninety-eight thousand people die every year as a result of medical errors in hospitals. Staph infections are seen in approximately seventy-five thousand people each year. Communicating effectively with medical professionals is essential to patient safety awareness.

Many patients think that their doctor has all the answers to every question or medical condition. In this era of specialization, it is essential that consumers take responsibility for their own health. Know your problem, research your problem, look at your alternatives, and talk to each medical professional in an informed manner.

Patient Safety Tips

Here are some tips to help keep you safe:

- ☐ Be a proactive, vocal, concerned, and involved consumer in matters relating to your health and that of your family.
- ☐ Question all procedures and medications.
- ☐ Research the medical problem that you have to deal with.
- ☐ Prepare for your visit with the doctor or nurse by making a list of questions.
- ☐ Insist that the doctor take the time to answer each of your questions in lay terms.
- ☐ Get a copy of all your medical records, including X-rays, and keep them with you.
- ☐ Ask the doctor how necessary a recommended operation or procedure is.
- ☐ Ask what the alternatives to the recommended operation or procedure are.
- ☐ Ask what the risks of the operation or procedure are.
- ☐ Ask what the expected results of the operation or procedure are.
- ☐ Ask what you might expect in recovery.
- ☐ Research who is the best doctor and the best hospital for a procedure or operation.
- ☐ Ask for referrals and doctor references.
- ☐ Research who is delivering the anesthesia. Be sure to speak with the doctor and ask about procedures. Tell him or her about any allergies you may have and about side effects.
- ☐ Be sure you have at least three opinions before you proceed with an operation.

☐ If you have gone to the hospital or clinic for an operation or procedure, be sure you have a person with you who knows about your condition so all treatment can be monitored.

☐ If you are going to a doctor to discuss a serious problem, be sure someone is with you to listen to the report and recommendations.

Consumers of health care often feel reluctant to ask for a referral to the best provider for a specific problem. Remember that you may have one chance at the correct procedure, the right medical care provider, and the best hospital for a procedure that could be life threatening.

Severe Acute Respiratory Syndrome (SARS)

SARS is a serious and contagious respiratory illness that has recently been reported in Asia, North America, and Europe. Symptoms include a fever greater than 100.4° F, chills, headache, discomfort, body aches, mild respiratory symptoms, and a cough after two to seven days, sometimes requiring mechanical ventilation. The cause of SARS is unknown, but a type of coronavirus is suspected. Apparently SARS is spread through droplet transmission in air or on contaminated objects. The incubation period is usually from two to seven days and may be up to ten days. Notify your doctor immediately if you or your family members suspect that you may have SARS. Prevention of SARS should include regular hand washing with antibacterial soap and water. Until further notice, postpone trips to countries where cases are reported For more detailed information, check the following sites, which are updated daily: <www.cdc.gov/ncidod/sars/> and <www.who.int/csr/sars/en/>.

Conclusion

This book has offered tips for making your home, your community, and the external world a safer place to live.

Today, threats to safety have become more real. We have seen how precious life is and how tragic it is when life is taken away from us. We have become more conscious of the safety of our loved ones and ourselves—not only when boarding an airplane or during a tornado warning, but also when living in our homes, taking care of our children, eating, going to school, participating in recreational activities, even celebrating a holiday. Our goal should be to do everything we can to deal with, prevent, and mitigate threats to our safety. In this respect, ensuring one's safety in the personal realm is just as much of a concern as in the external world.

Use this opportunity to take charge of your safety. Develop a family disaster plan, so that each member of your family will know what to do whether they are at home, at work, at school, or in a vehicle if tragedy strikes again.

Resources

AARP: www.aarp.org

American Academy of Pediatrics: www.aap.org

American Association of Poison Control Centers: www.aapcc.org

American National Standards Institute   www.ansi.org

American Red Cross: www.redcross.org

Centers for Disease Control and Prevention (CDC):   www.cdc.gov

Children's Hospital of Pittsburgh: www.chp.edu/besafe/index.php

Children's Safety, Consumer Federation of America: www.safechild.net

Consumer Product Safety Commission (CPSC):   www.cpsc.gov

Environmental Protection Agency (EPA):   www.epa.gov

Federal Aviation Administration (FAA):   www.faa.gov

Federal Bureau of Investigation (FBI):   www.fbi.gov

Federal Citizen Information Center: www.pueblo.gsa.gov

Federal Emergency Management Agency (FEMA):   www.fema.gov

Federal Trade Commission (FTC):   www.ftc.gov

First Gov for Consumers: www.consumer.gov

First Gov for Kids: www.kids.gov

Food Allergy Network: www.foodallergy.org

Food and Drug Administration (FDA):   www.fda.gov

Food Safety: www.foodsafety.gov

General Safety: www.safetyinfo.com

General Safety: www.safewithin.com

I'm Safe!:   www.imsafe.com

Institute for Business and Home Safety: www.ibhs.org

Internet Safety: www.safekids.com

Juvenile Products Manufacturers Association (JPMA):   www.jpma.org

National Center for Injury Prevention and Control: www.cdc.gov/ncipc/

National Highway Traffic Safety Administration (NHTSA):
   www.nhtsa.gov

National Inhalant Prevention Coalition: www.inhalants.org

National Institutes of Health (NIH):   www.nih.gov

National Safe Kids Campaign: www.safekids.org

National Safety Council: www.nsc.org

Partnership for Food Safety Education: www.fightbac.org

Poison Control Center National Hotline: 1-800-222-1222

Recall Information: www.safetyalerts.com

Safety Link: www.safetylink.com

Underwriters' Laboratories: www.ul.com

U.S. Department of Agriculture (USDA):   www.usda.gov

U.S. Department of Homeland Security: www.dhs.gov, www.ready.gov

U.S. Fire Administration: www.usfa.fema.gov

Washington, D.C., Emergency Management: dcema.dc.gov

White House: www.whitehouse.gov

Index